PLACES BEYOND

ERIK JOHANSSON

MAX STRÖM

For me, creating an image is like creating a place. A place that feels familiar, but with a twist that causes the viewer to stop short.

When I started creating these images, it was largely about experimenting to see how far I could distort reality without losing realism. Over time, the story has taken on more of a central role in my image-making. I now use colour and light more consistently to heighten the emotion and narrative. While much of the challenge is on the technical level, successfully capturing an entire story in a single image is equally important. The titles may provide a clue, but I want the images to speak for themselves.

Welcome to my world.

Erik Johansson

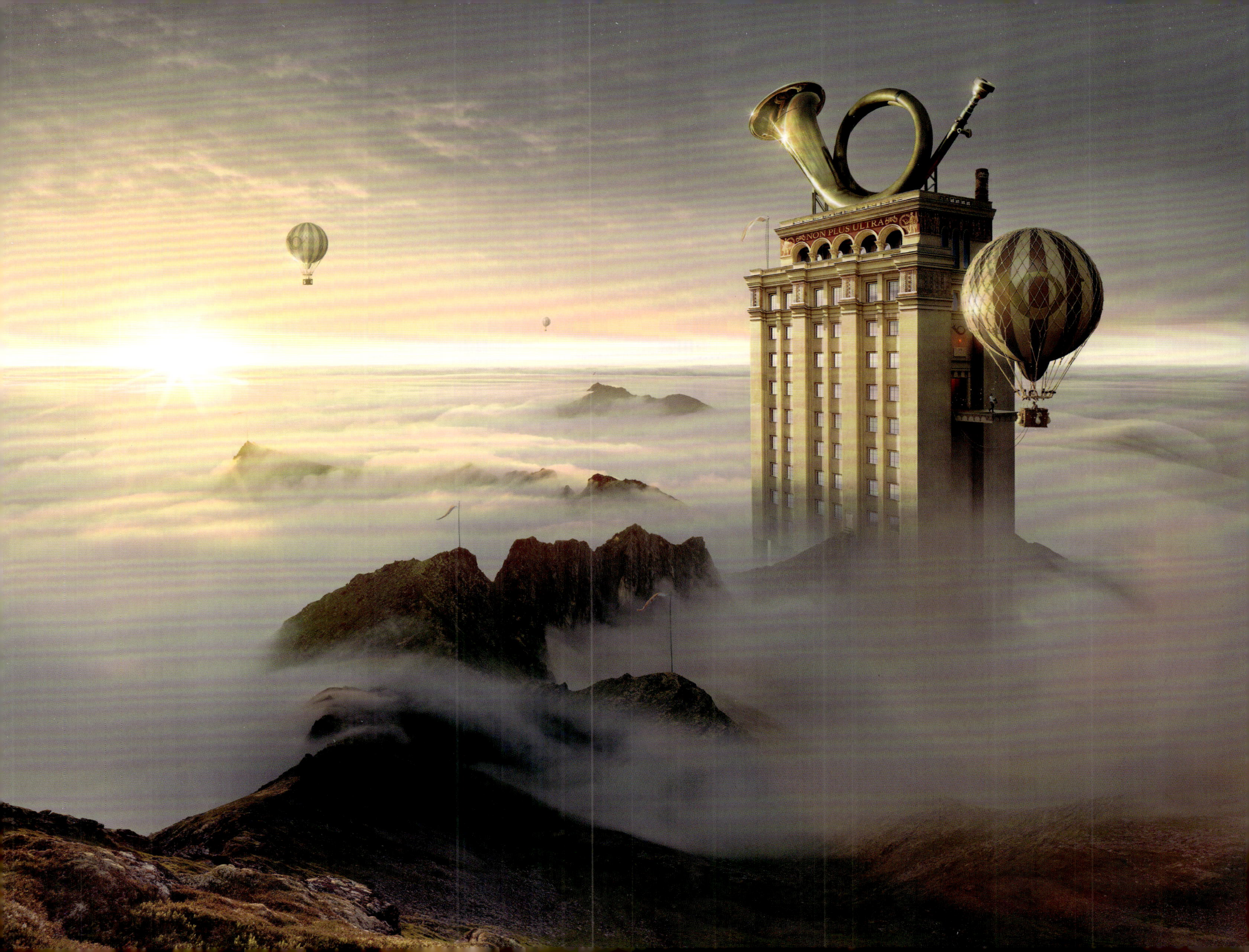
NON PLUS ULTRA

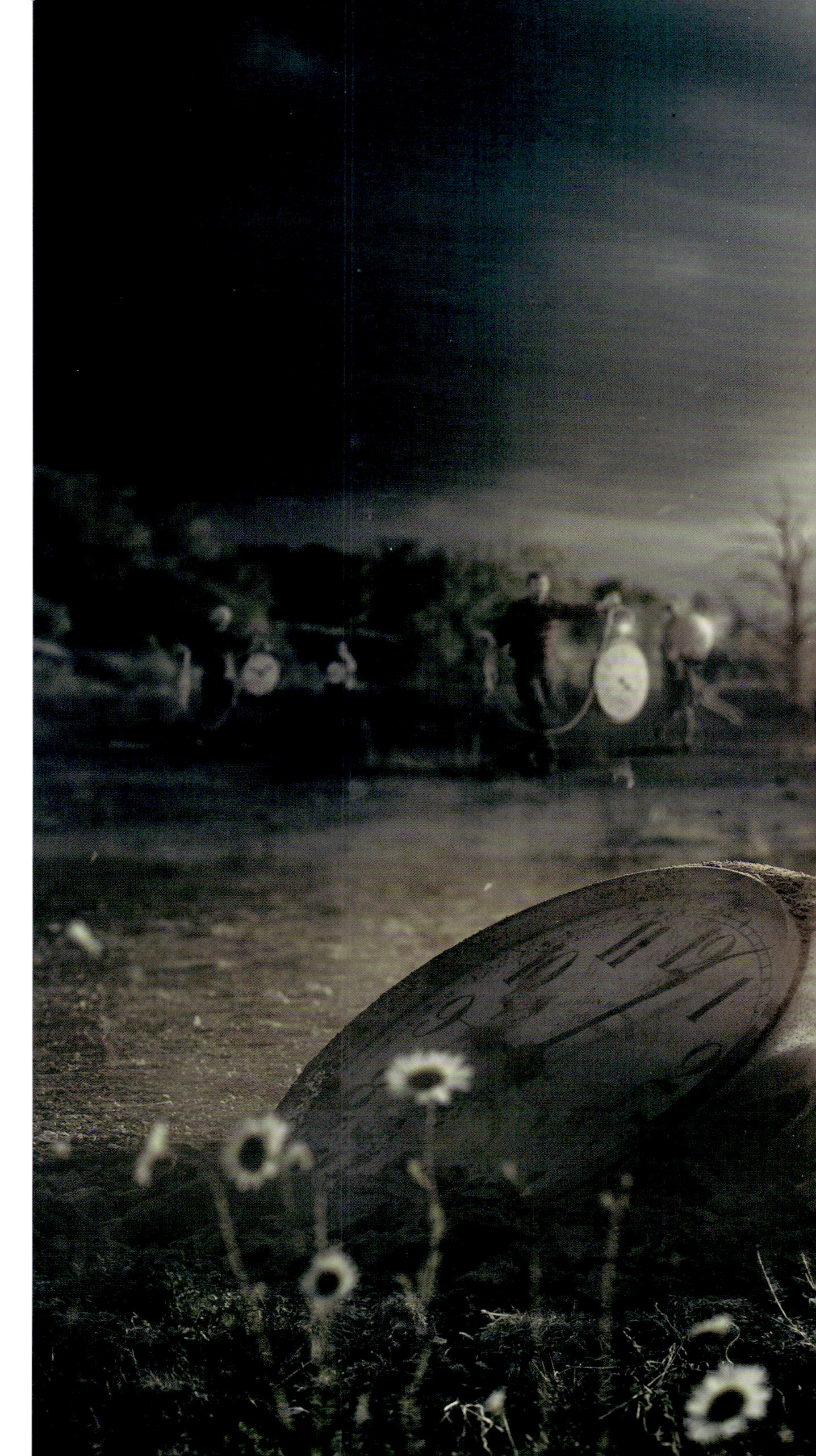

Give me Time

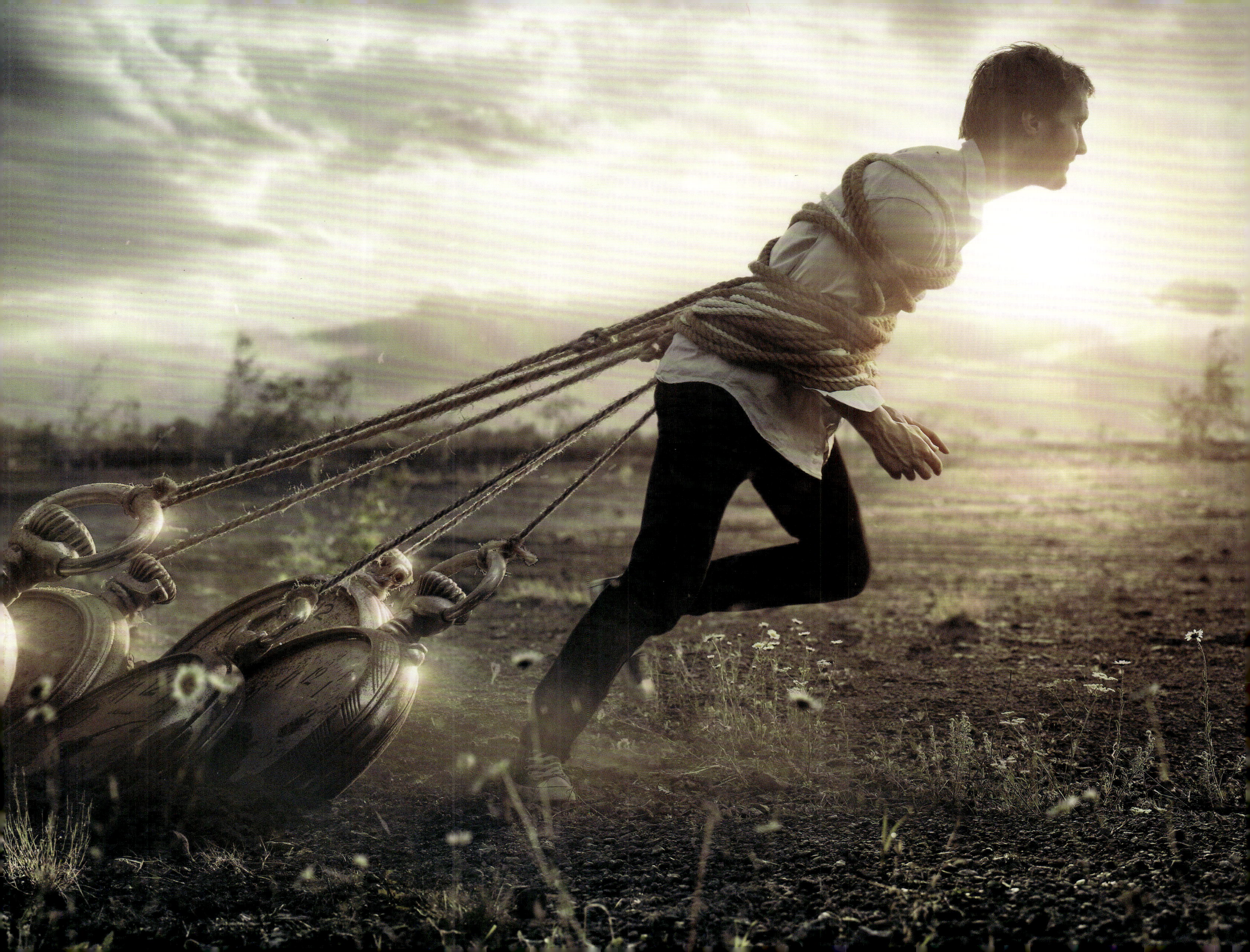

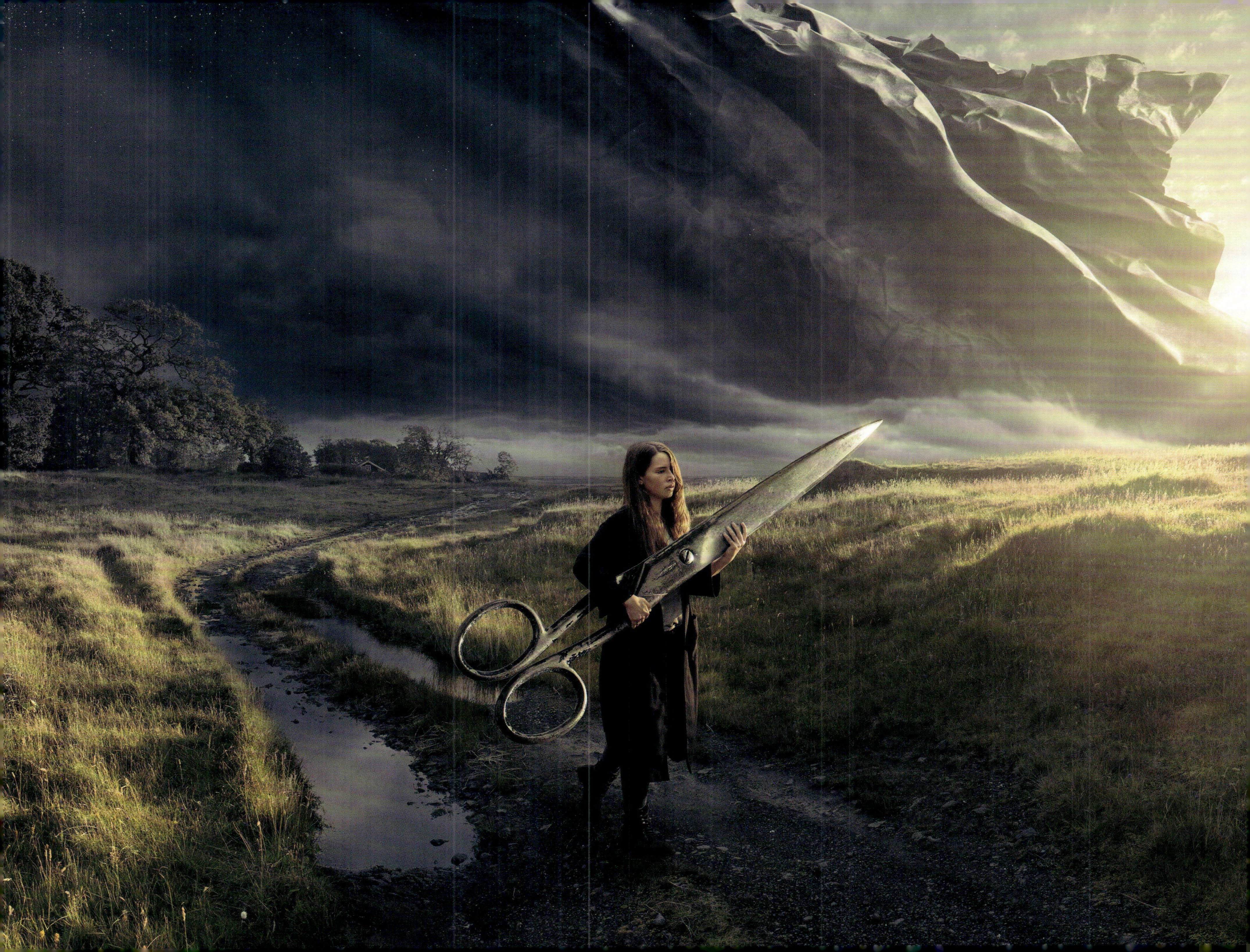

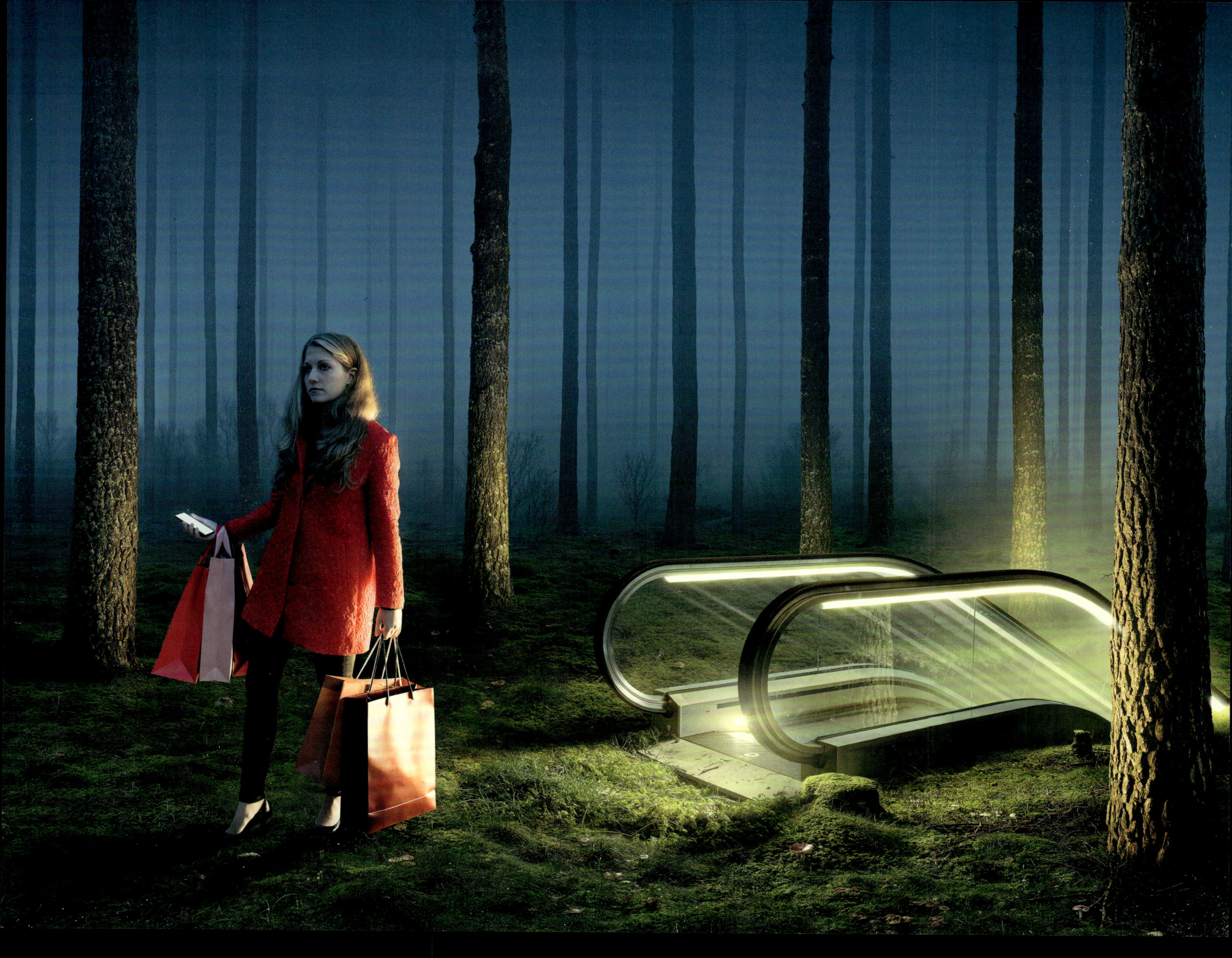

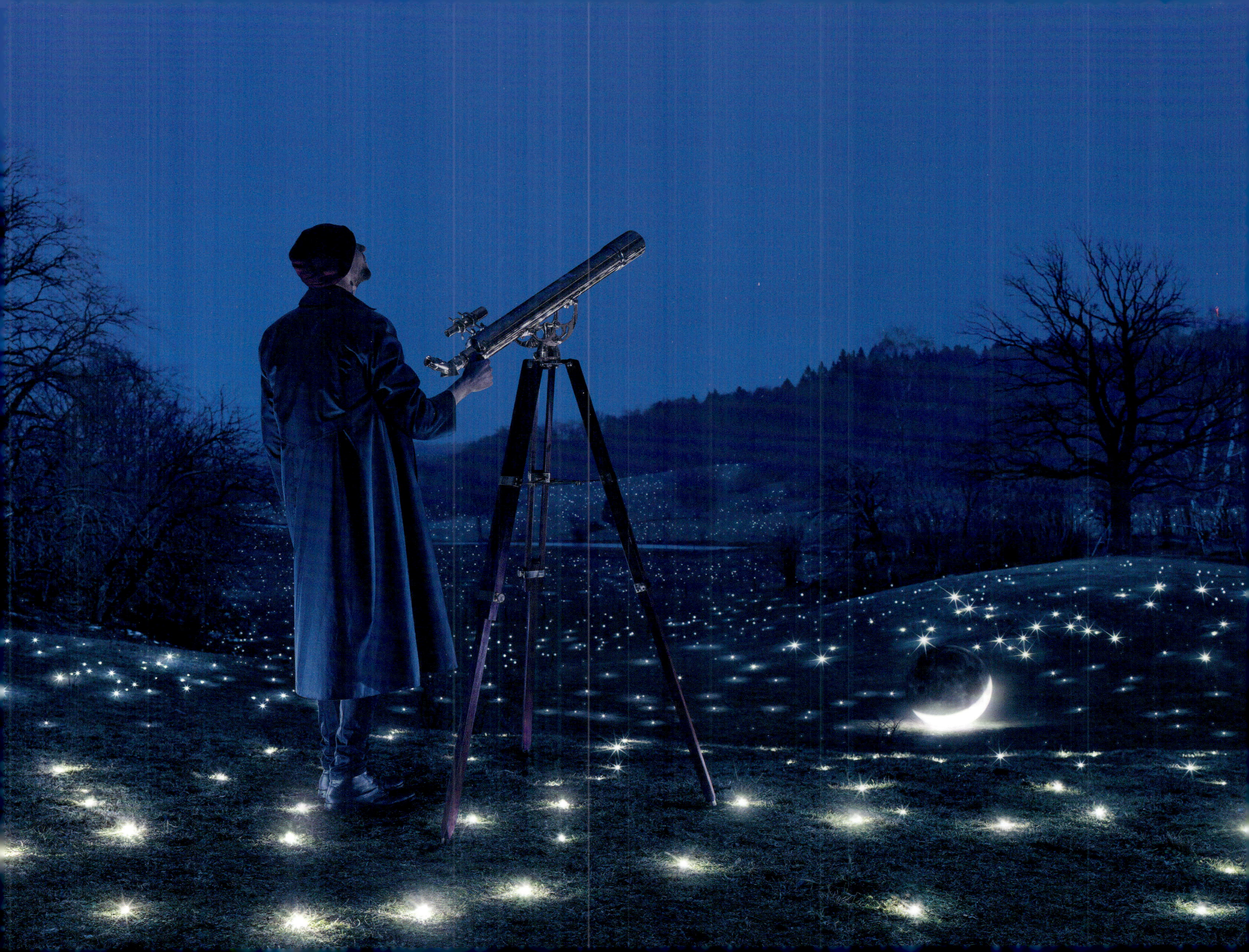

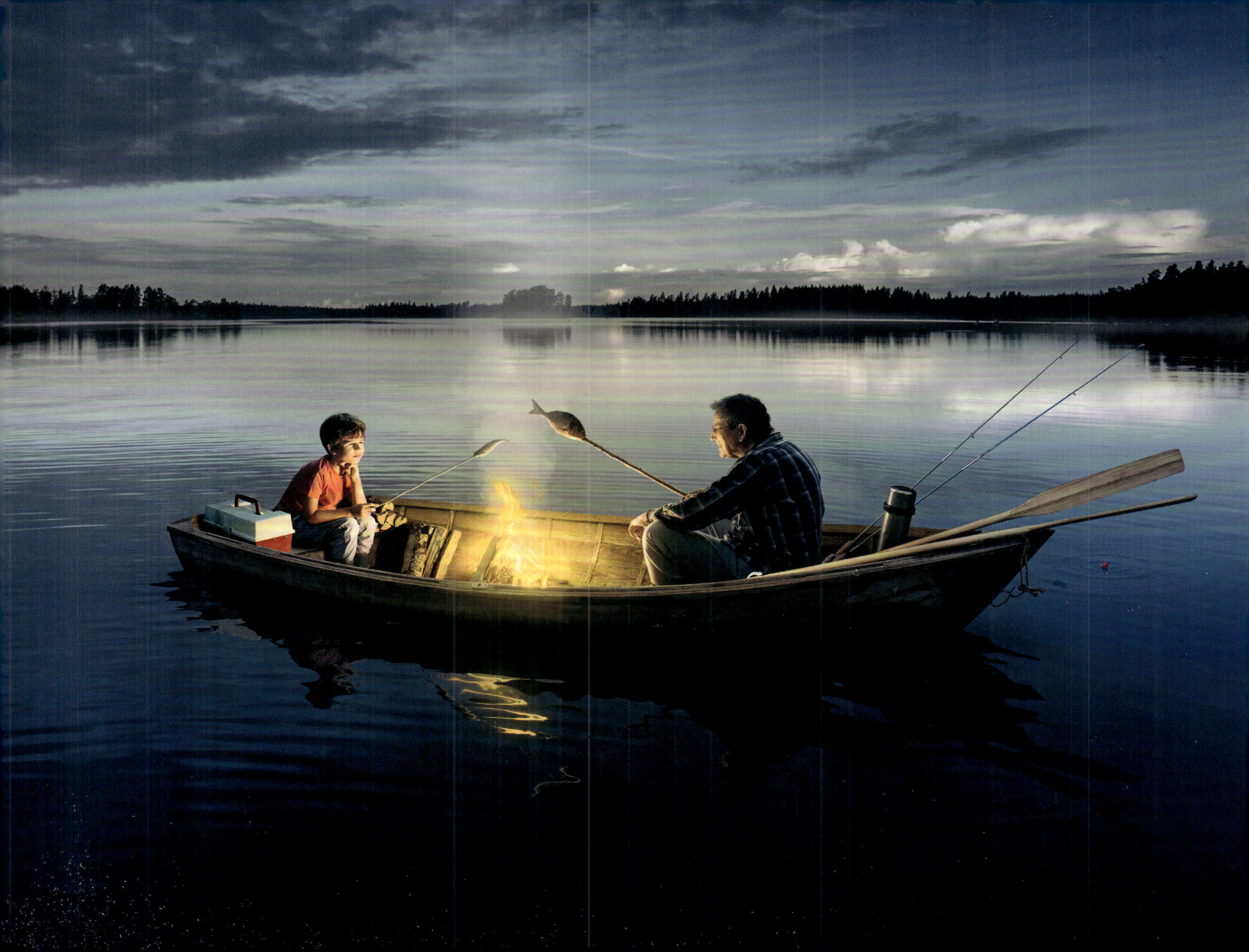

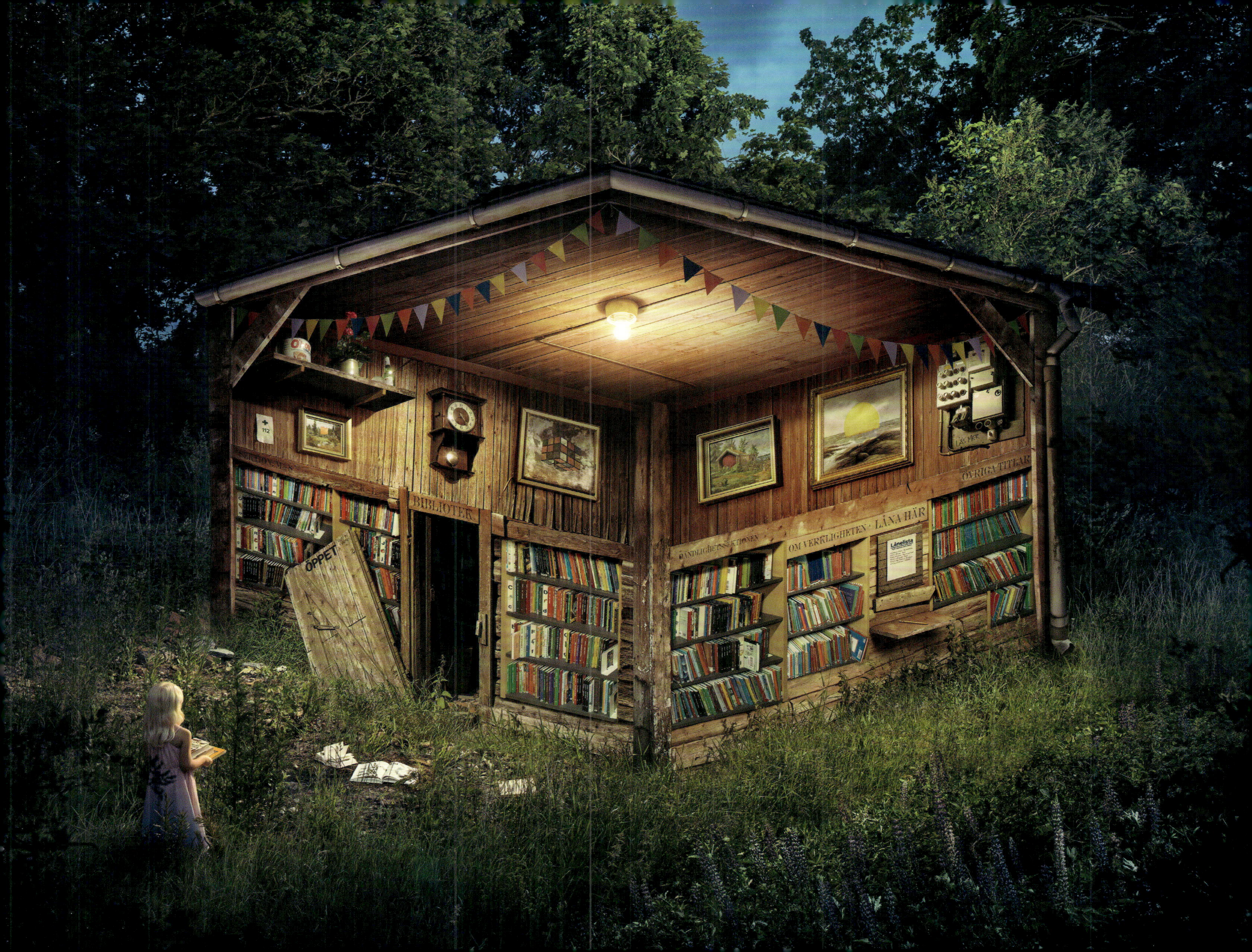
T12
BIBLIOTEK
ÖPPET
OÄNDLIGHETSSEKTIONEN
OM VERKLIGHETEN · LÅNA HÄR
ÖVRIGA TITLAR
LÄS HÄR
Lånelista

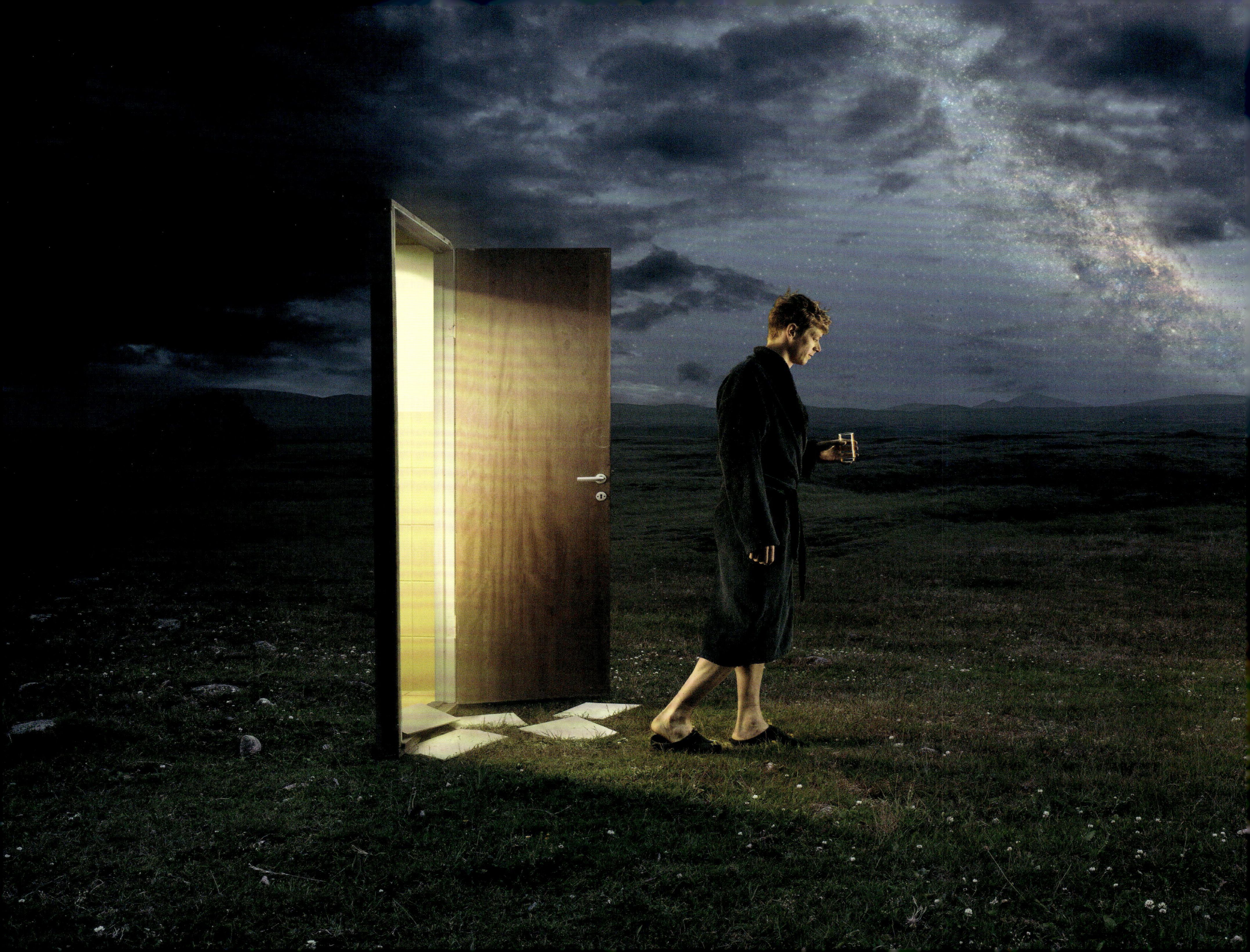

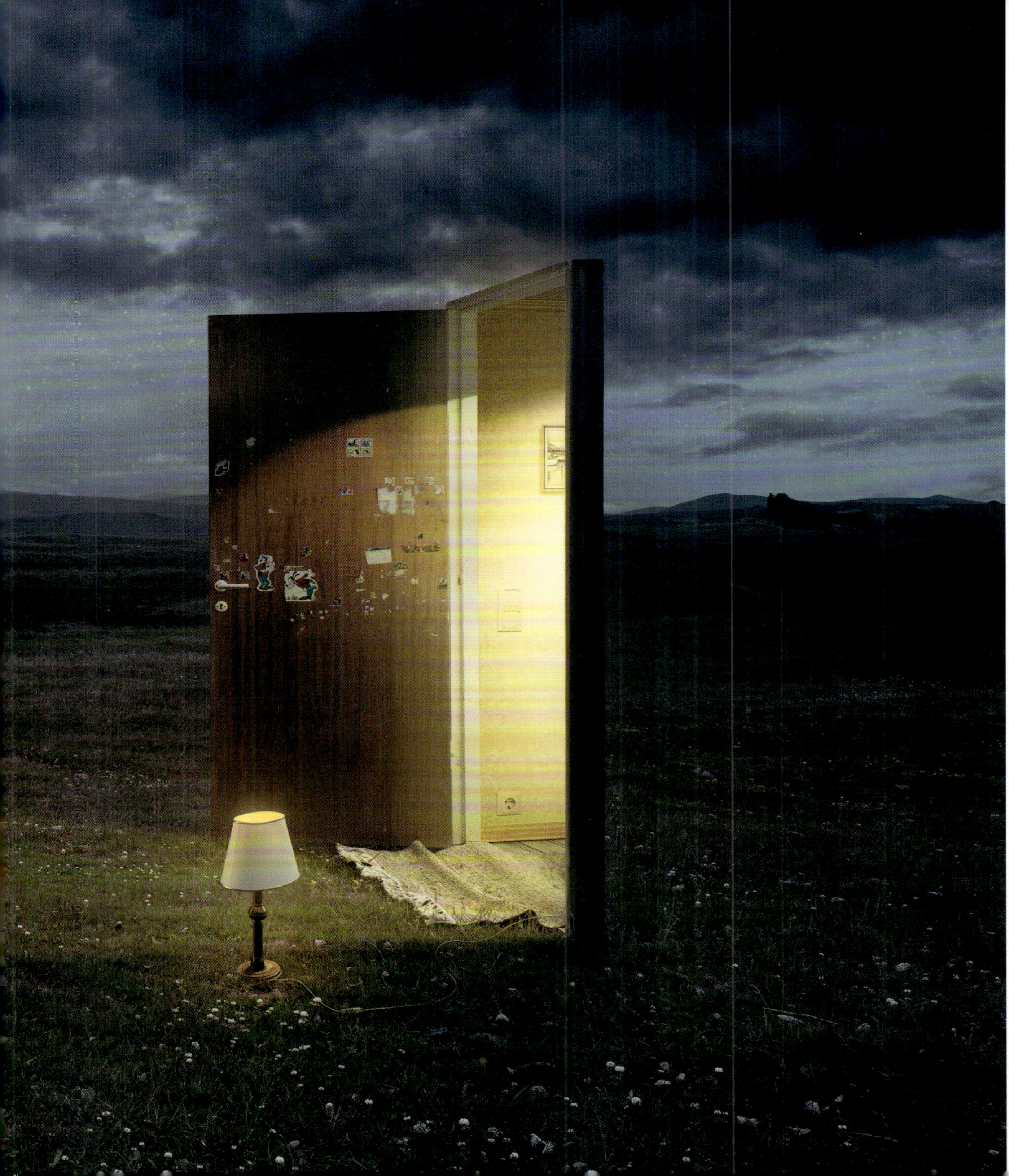

Dreamwalking

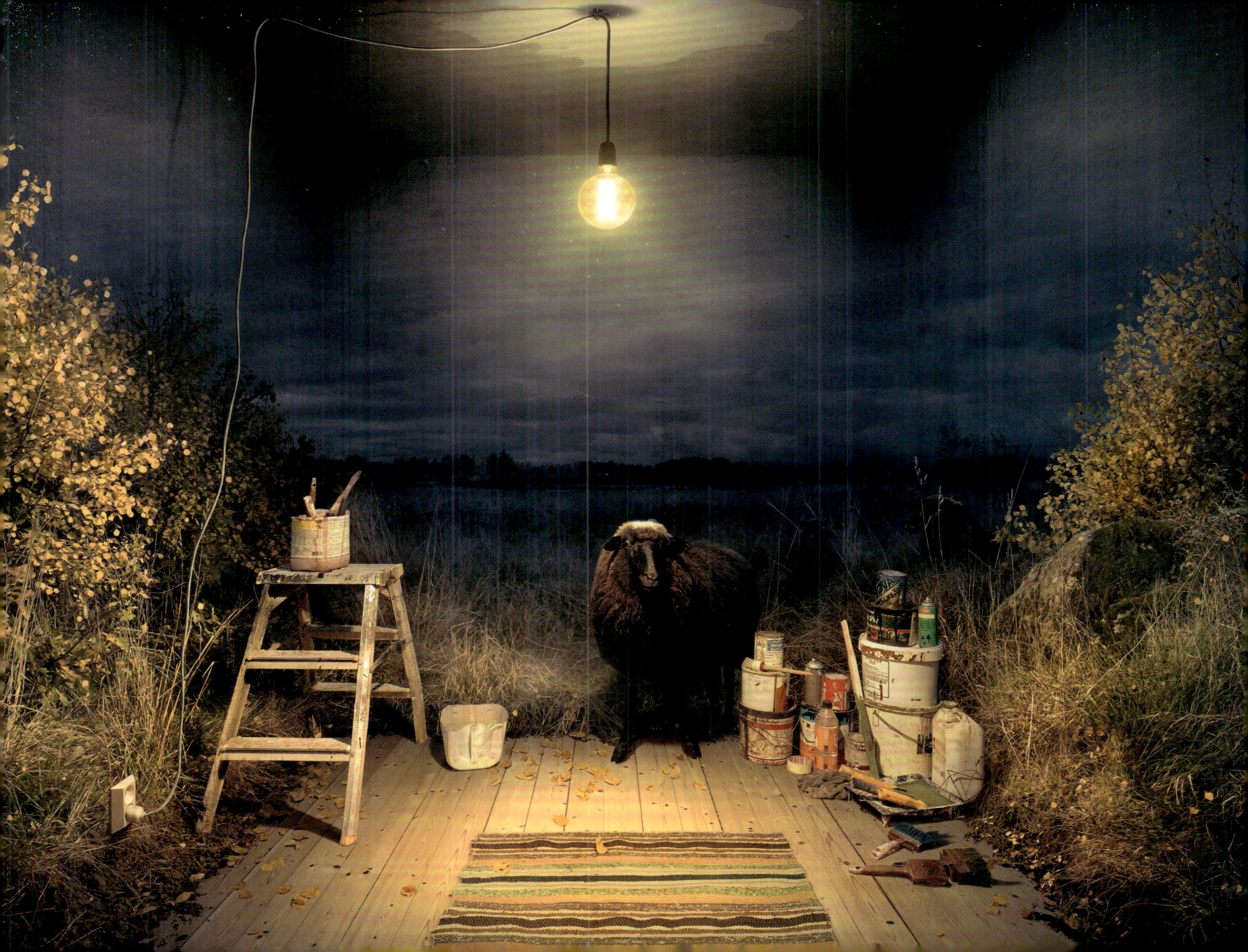

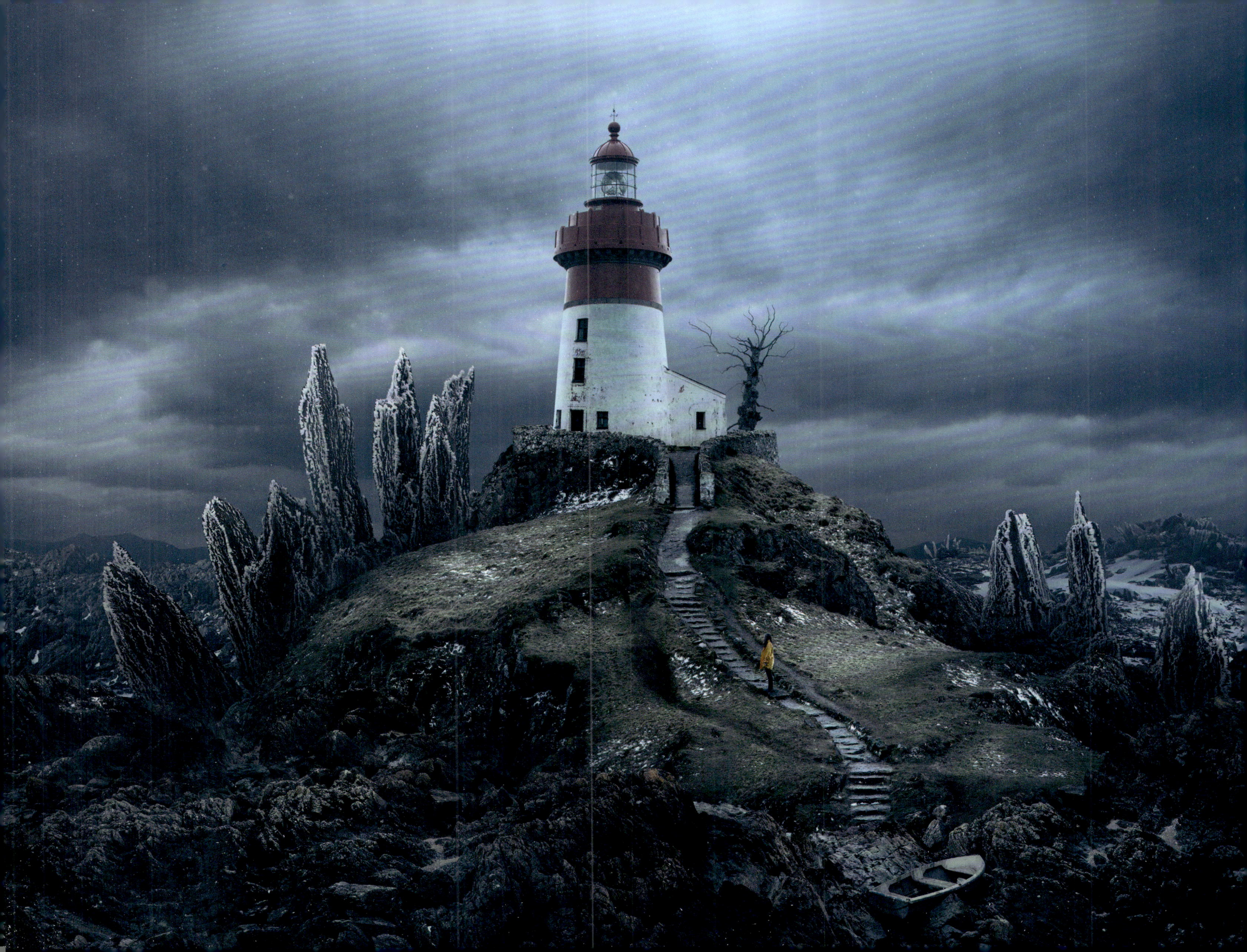

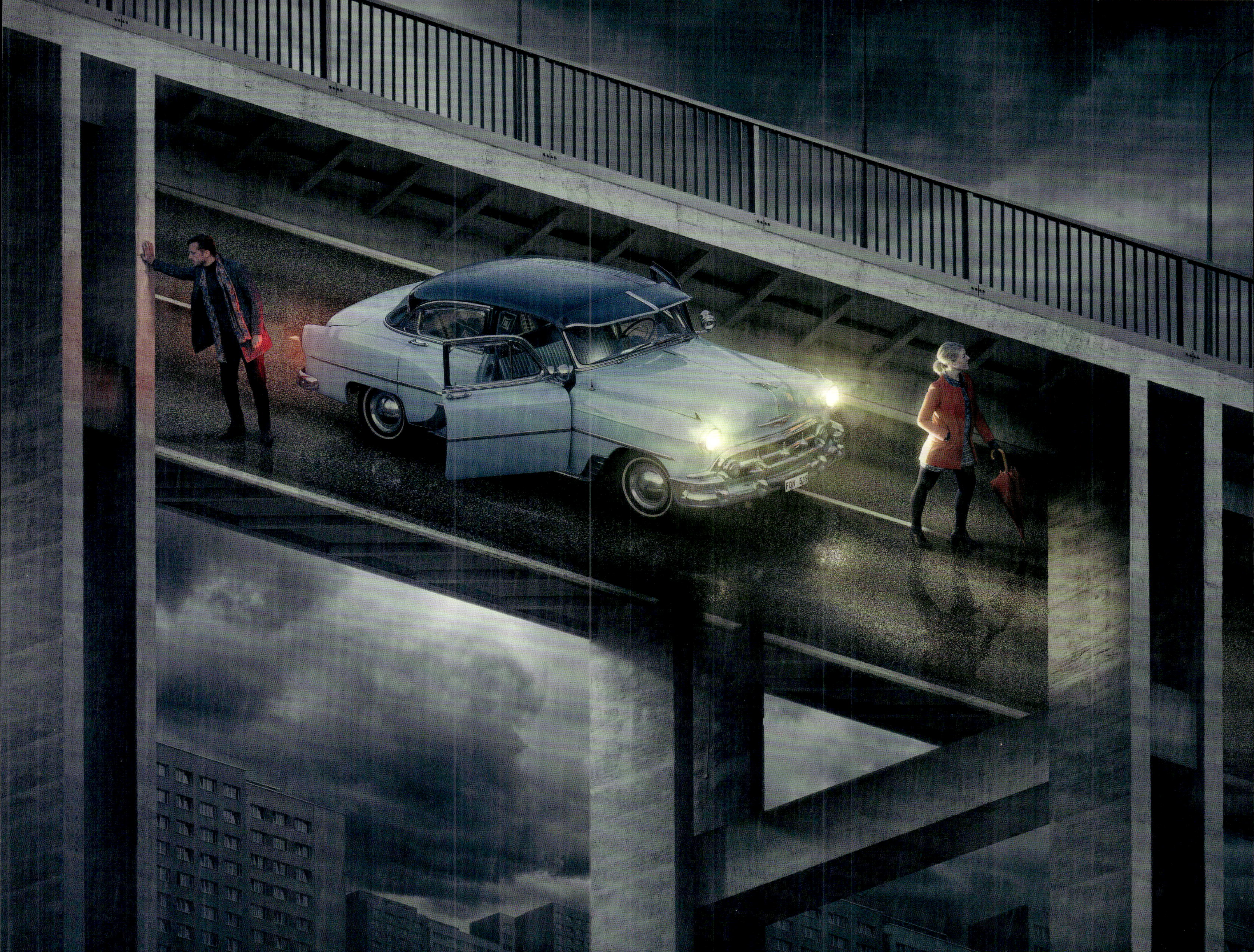

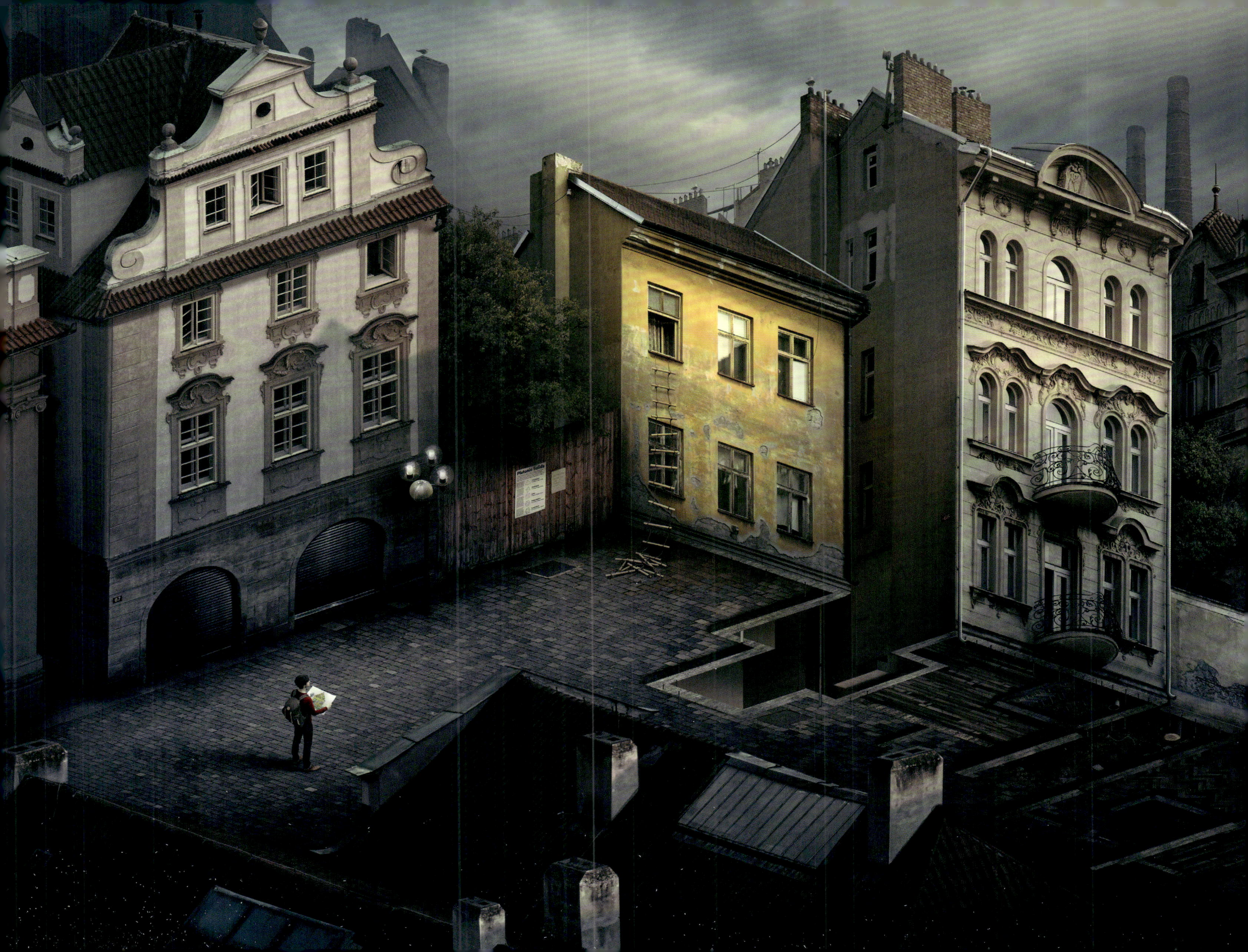

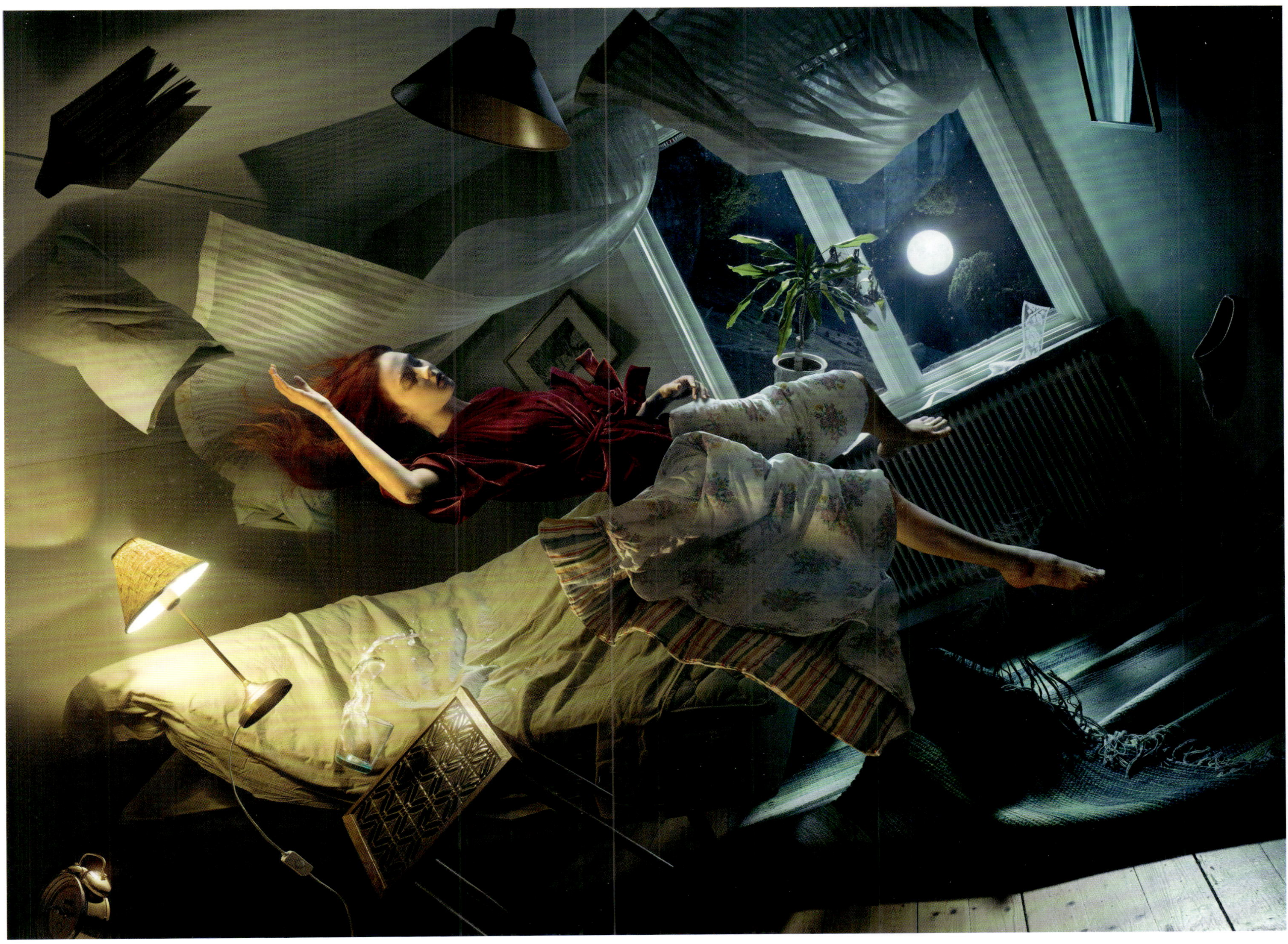

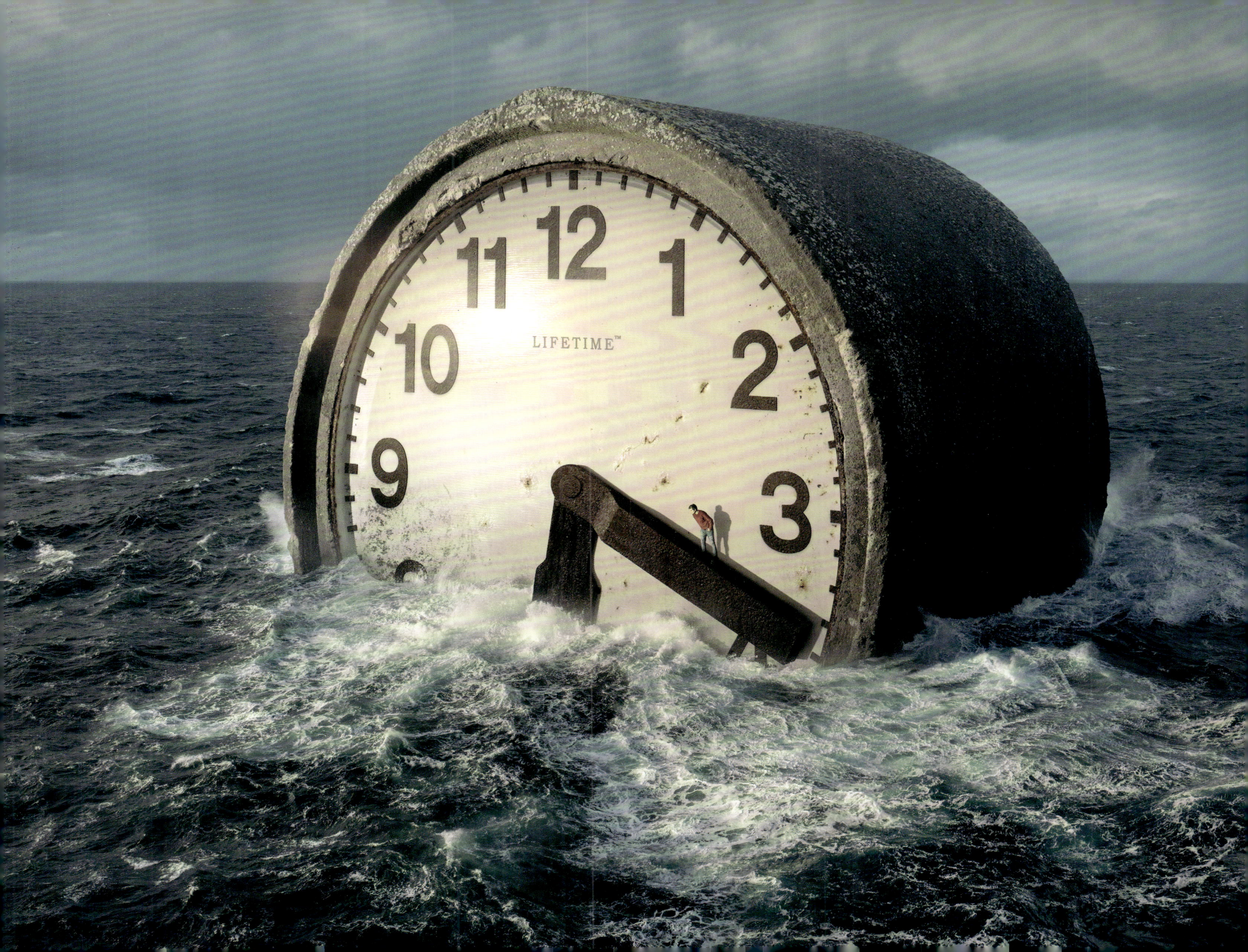

12
11
10
9
1
2
3
LIFETIME™

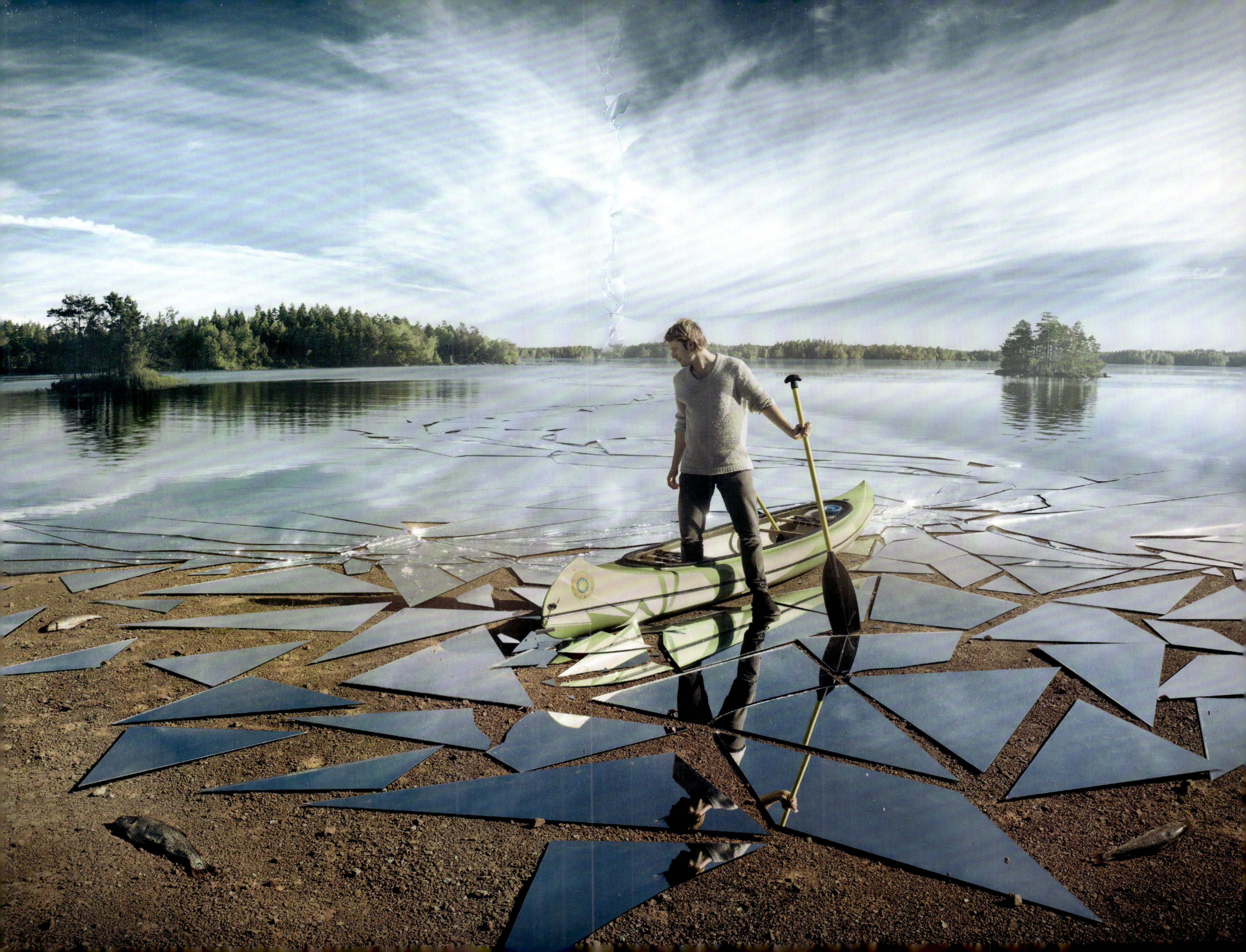

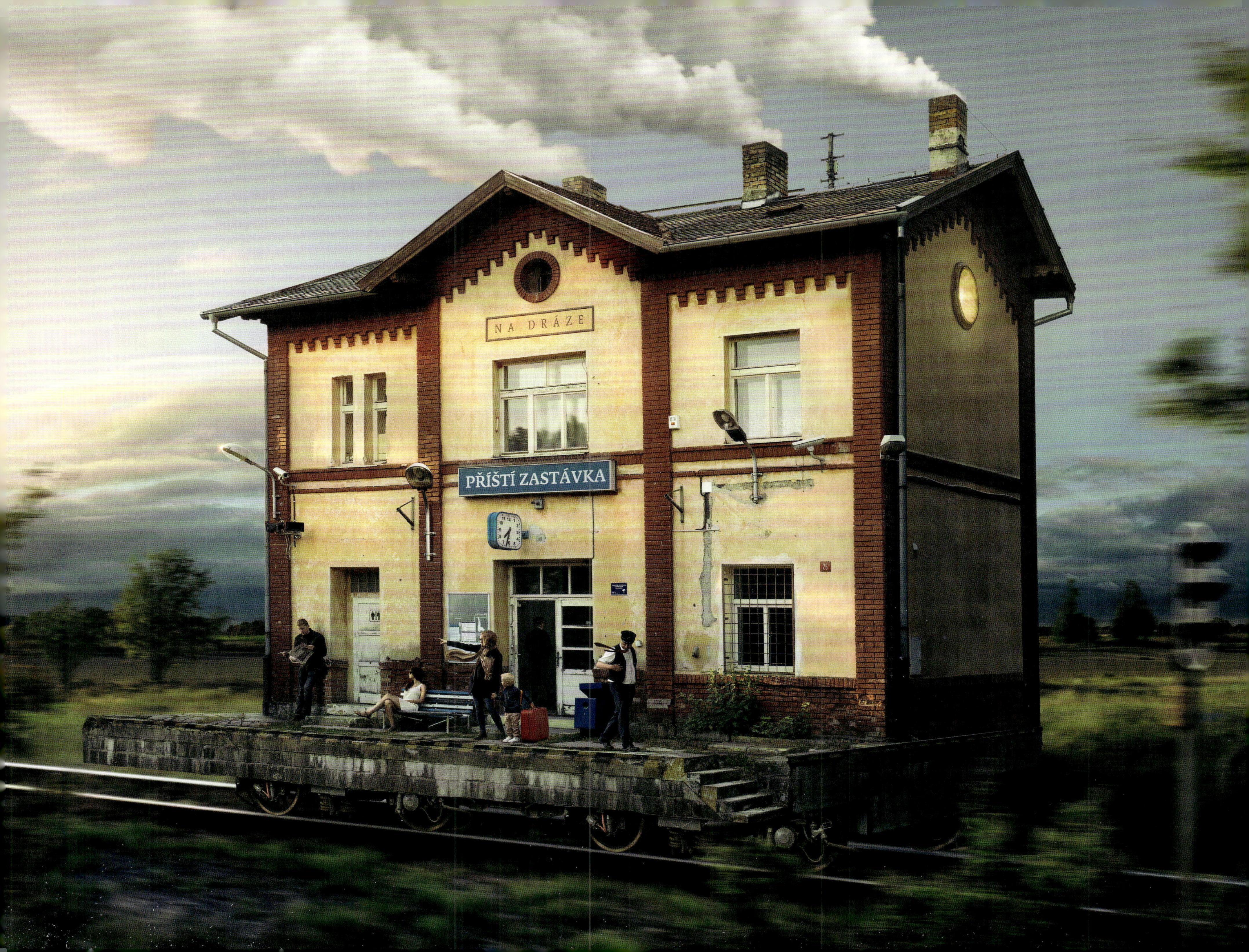

NA DRÁZE
PŘÍŠTÍ ZASTÁVKA

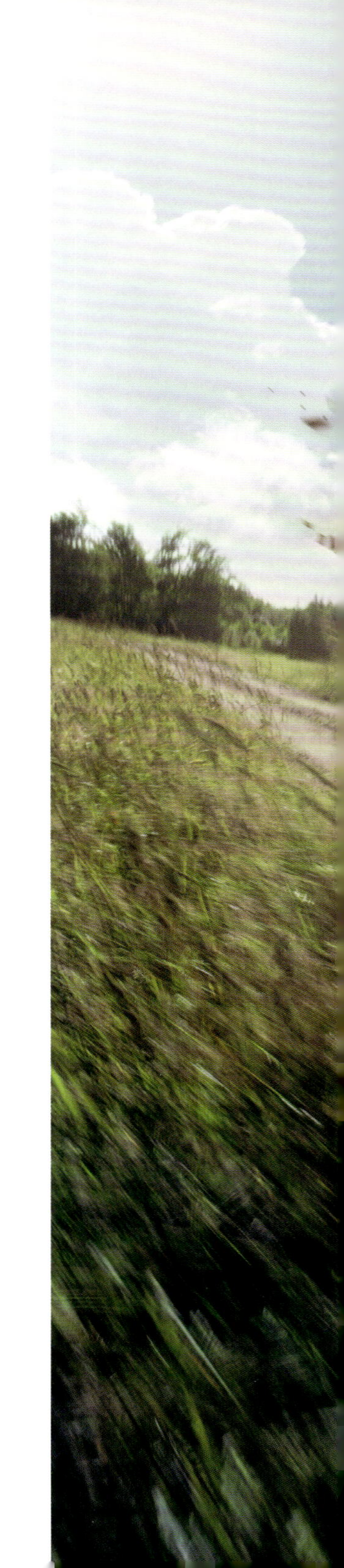

Looking Back

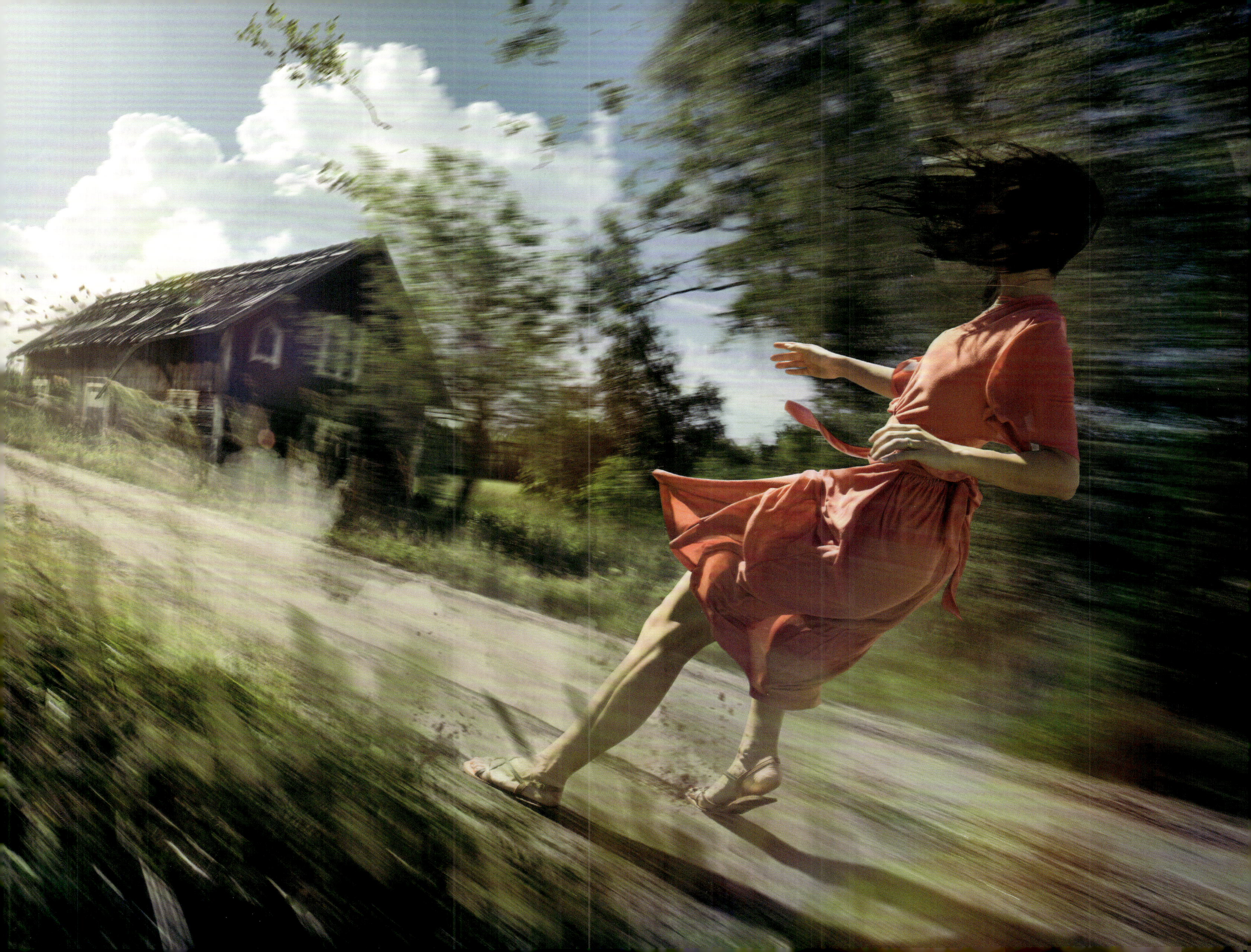

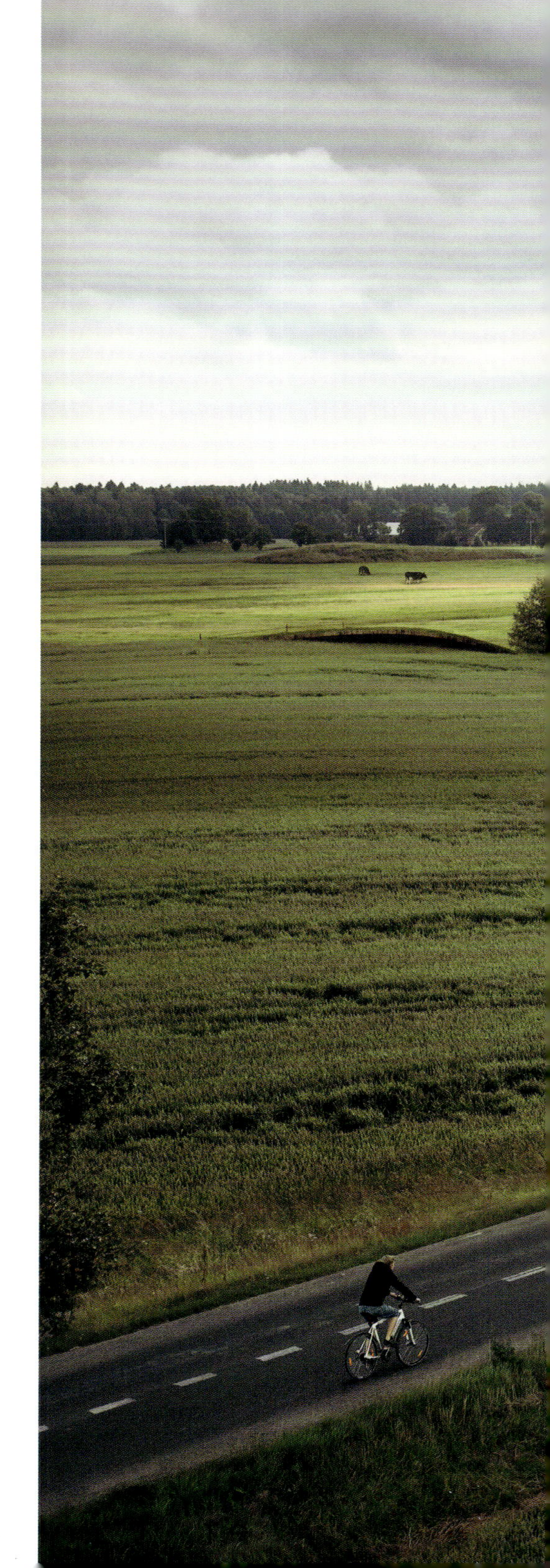

Cut & Fold

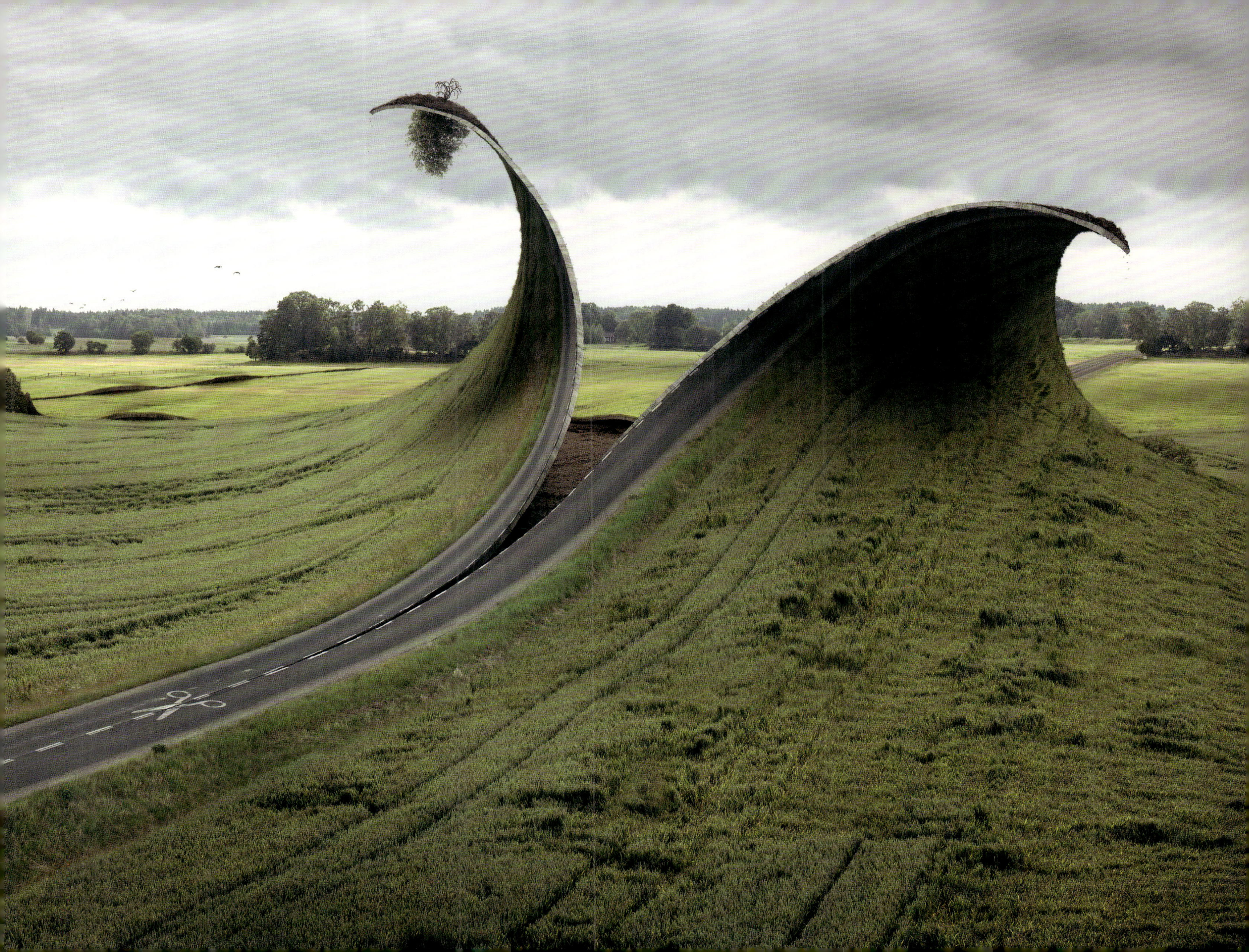

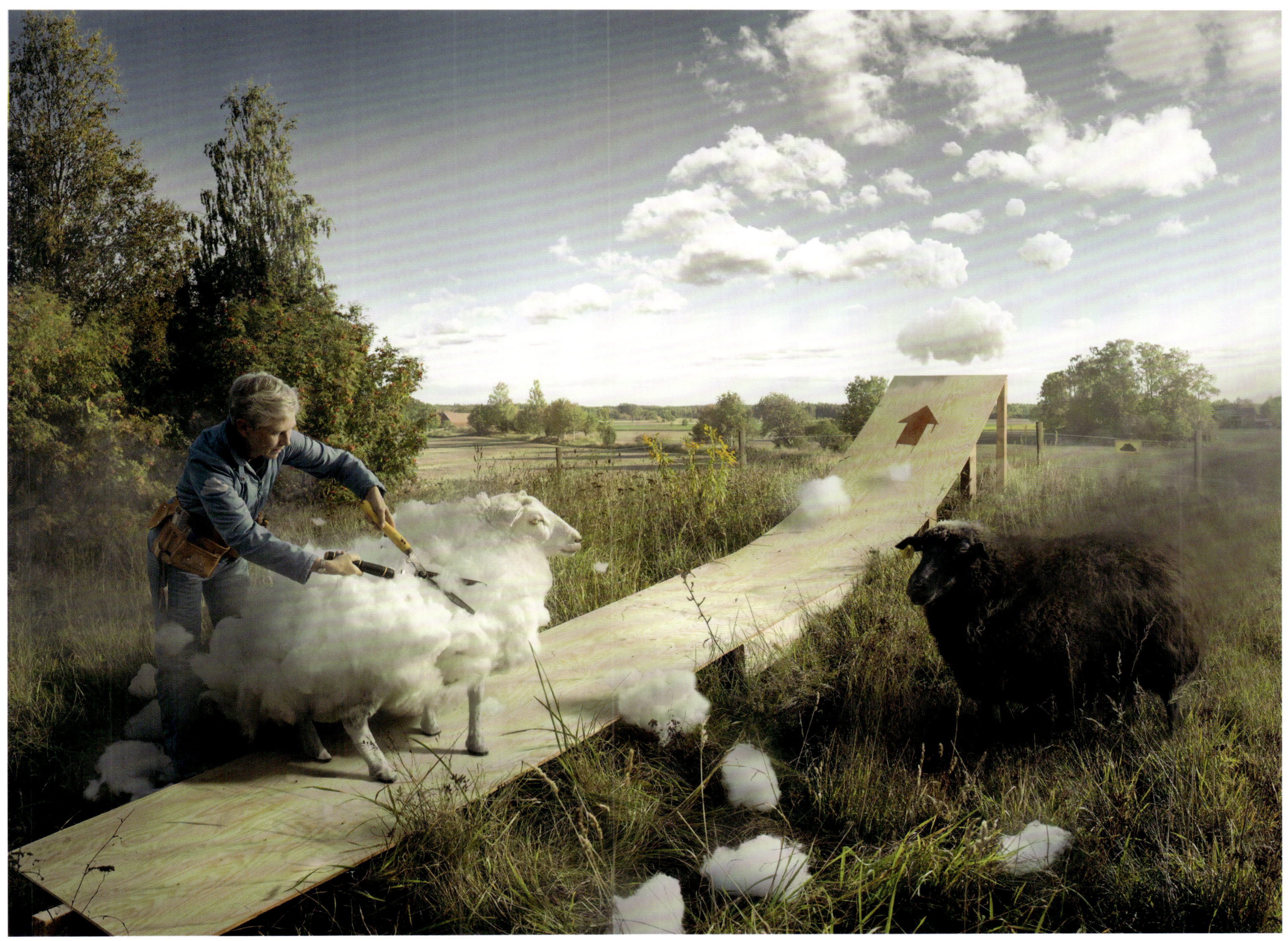

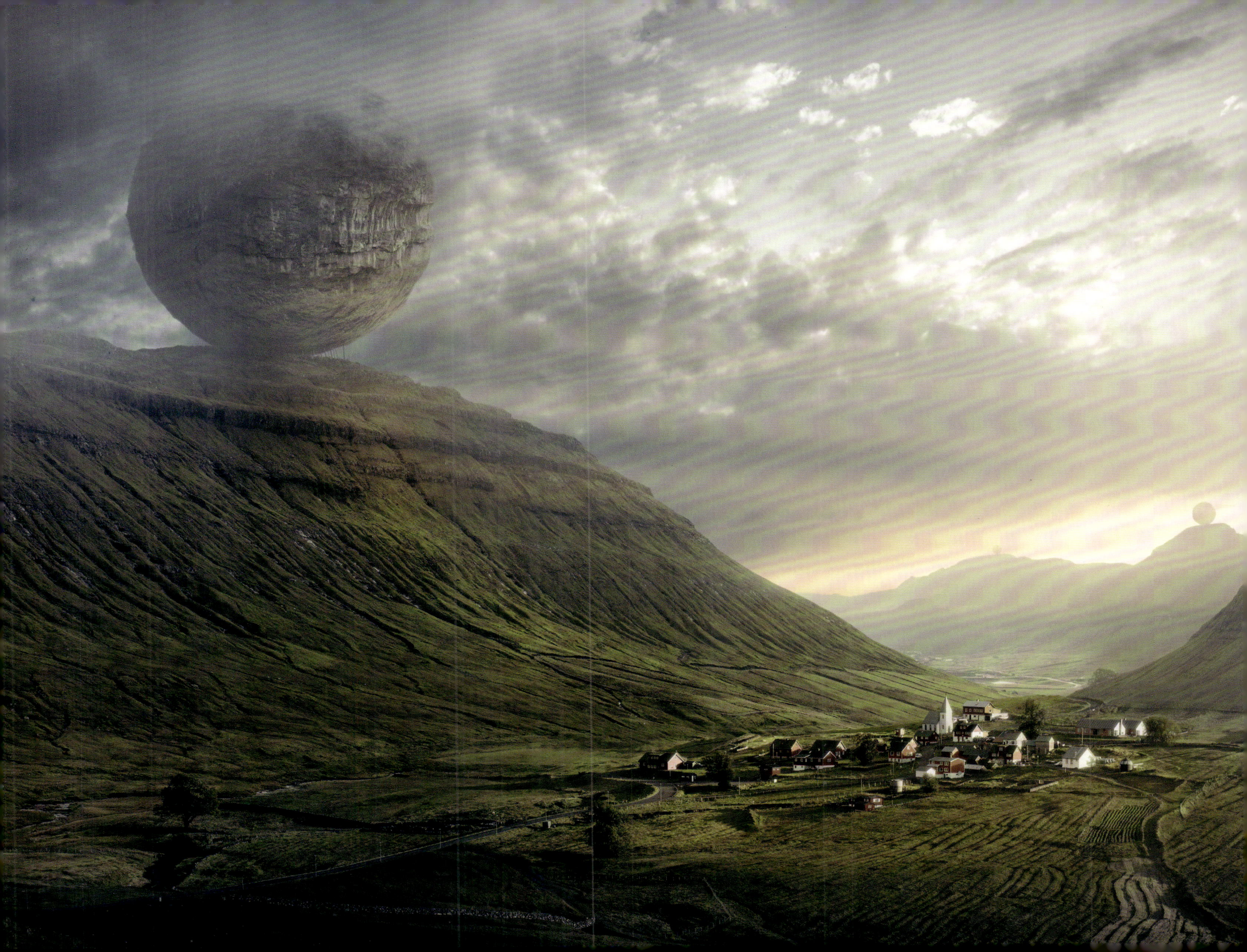

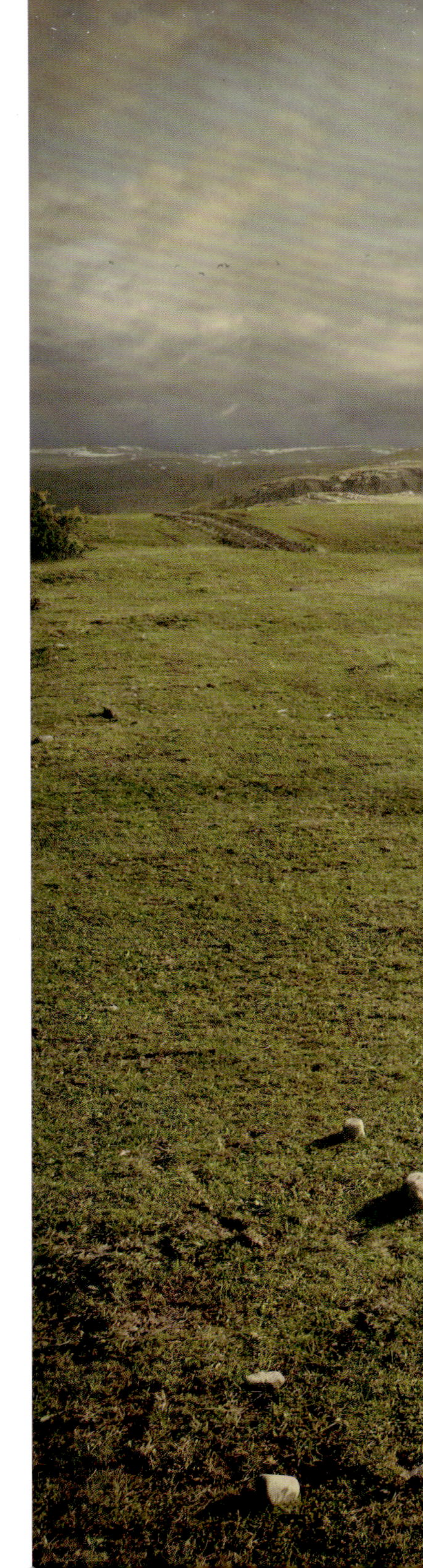

Groundbreaking

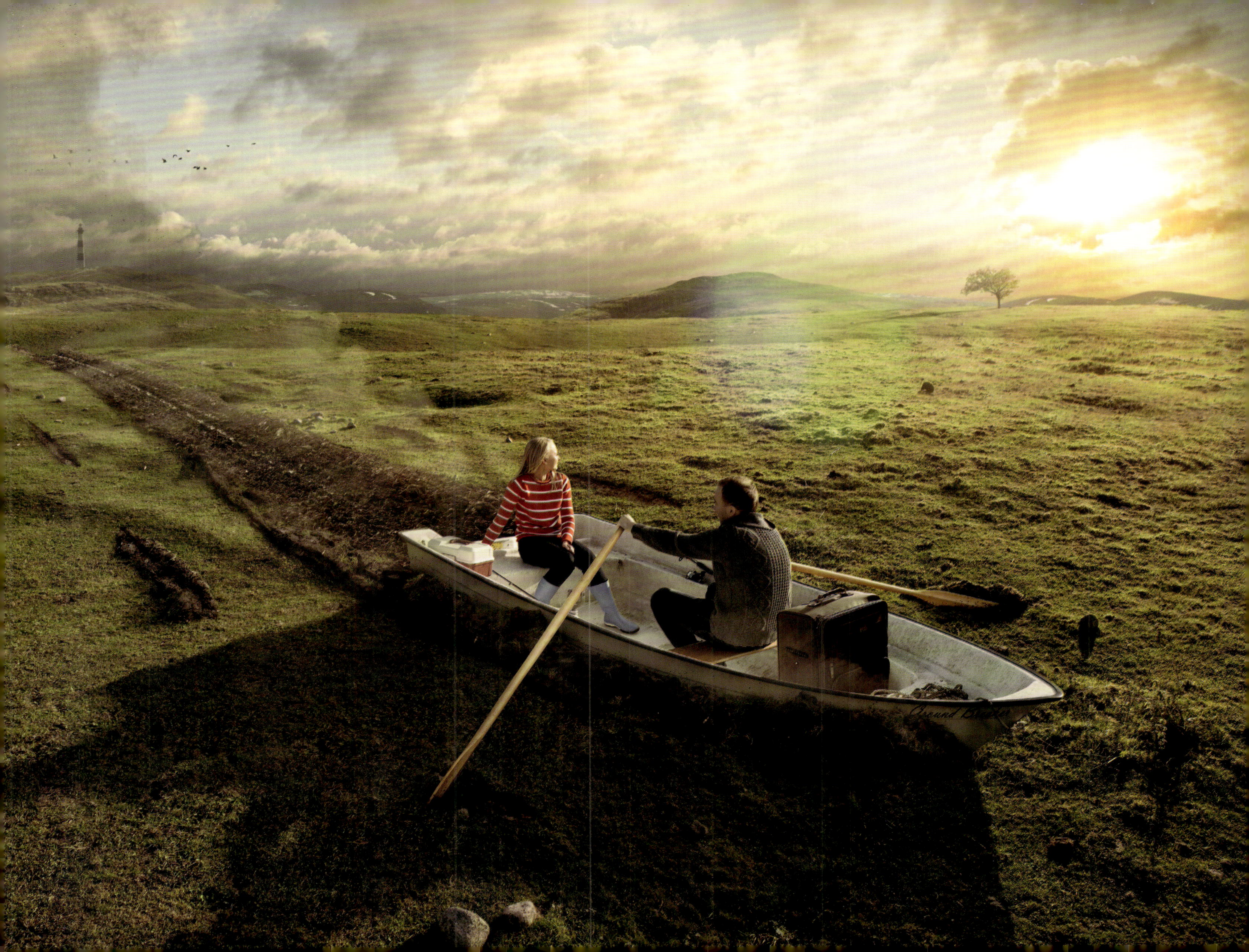

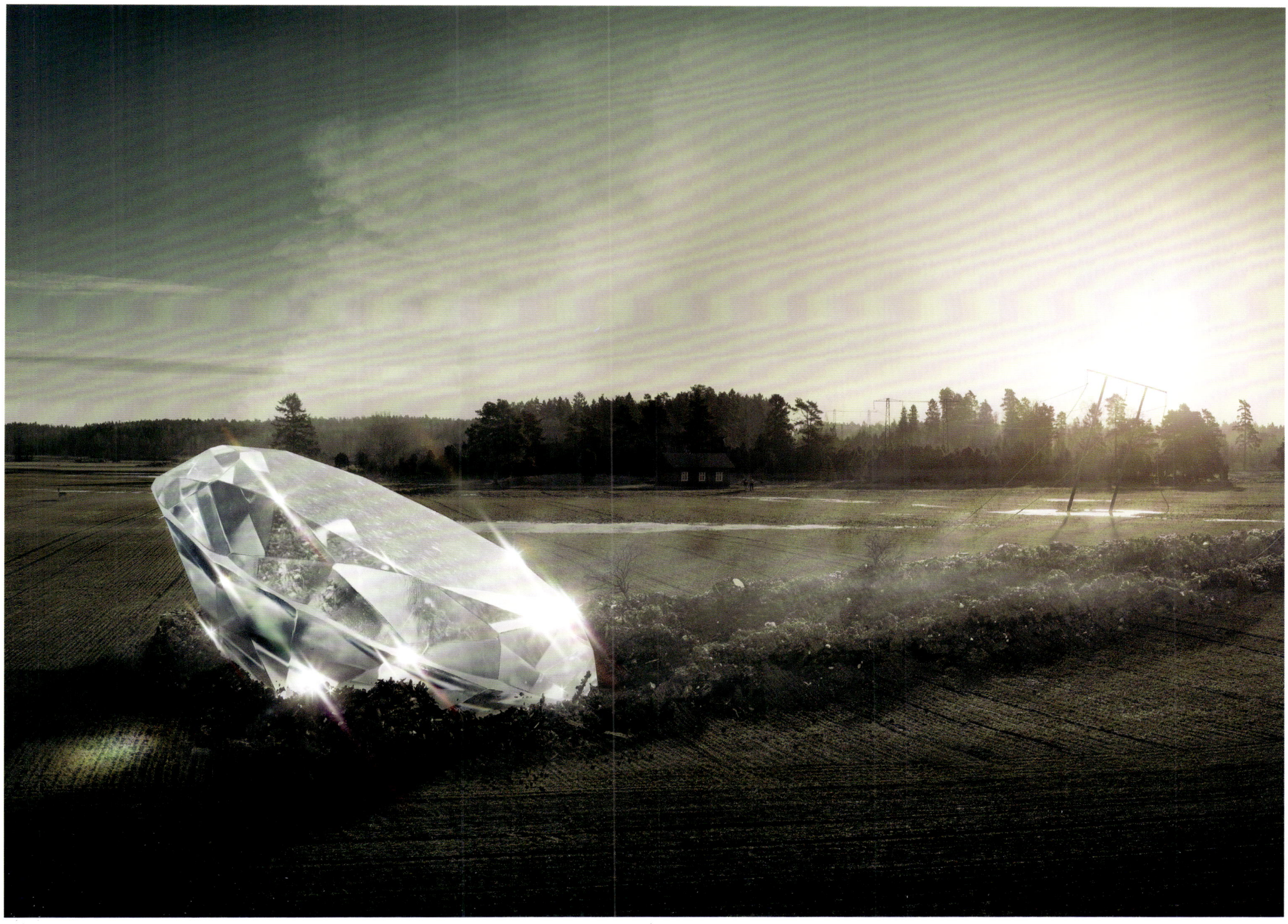

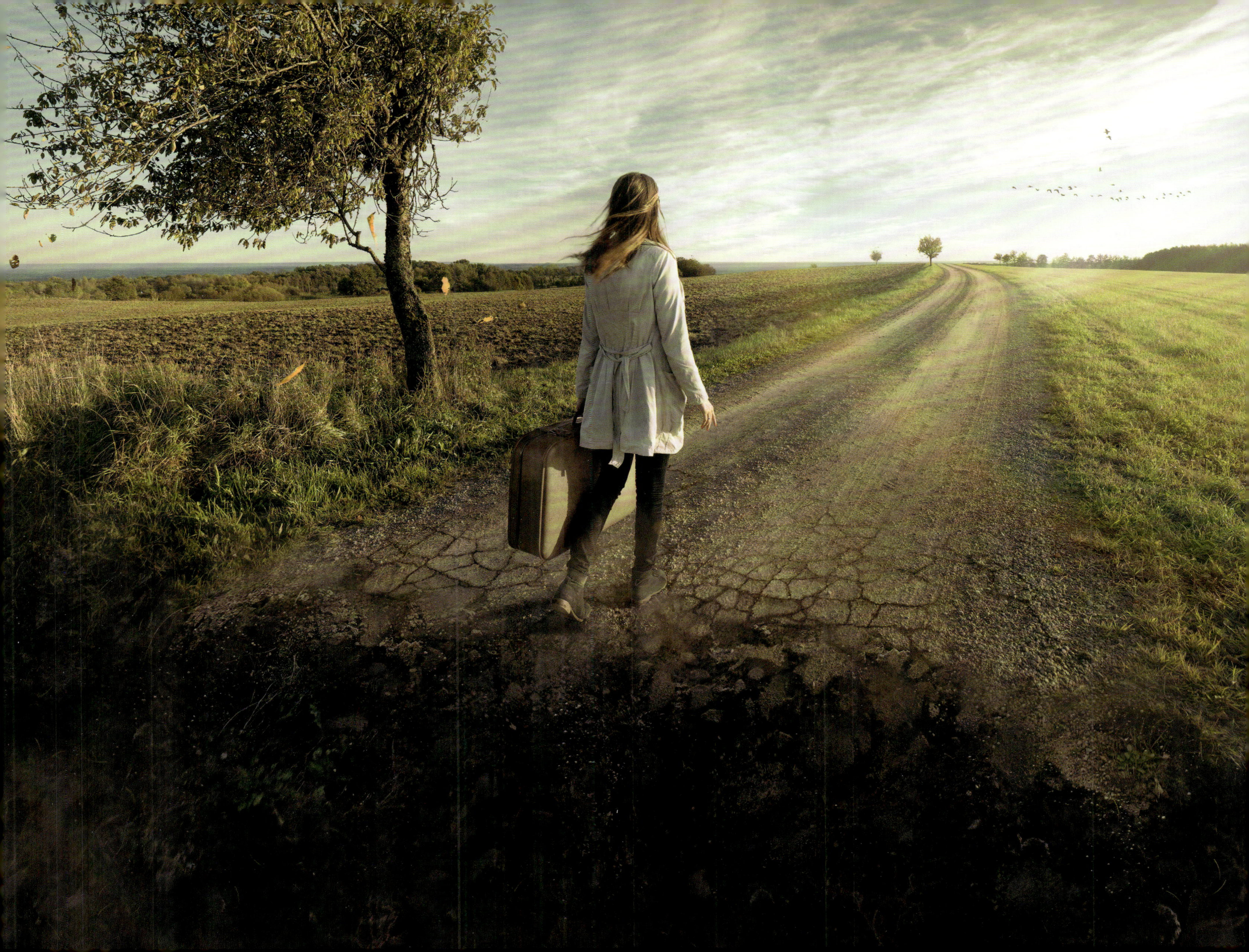

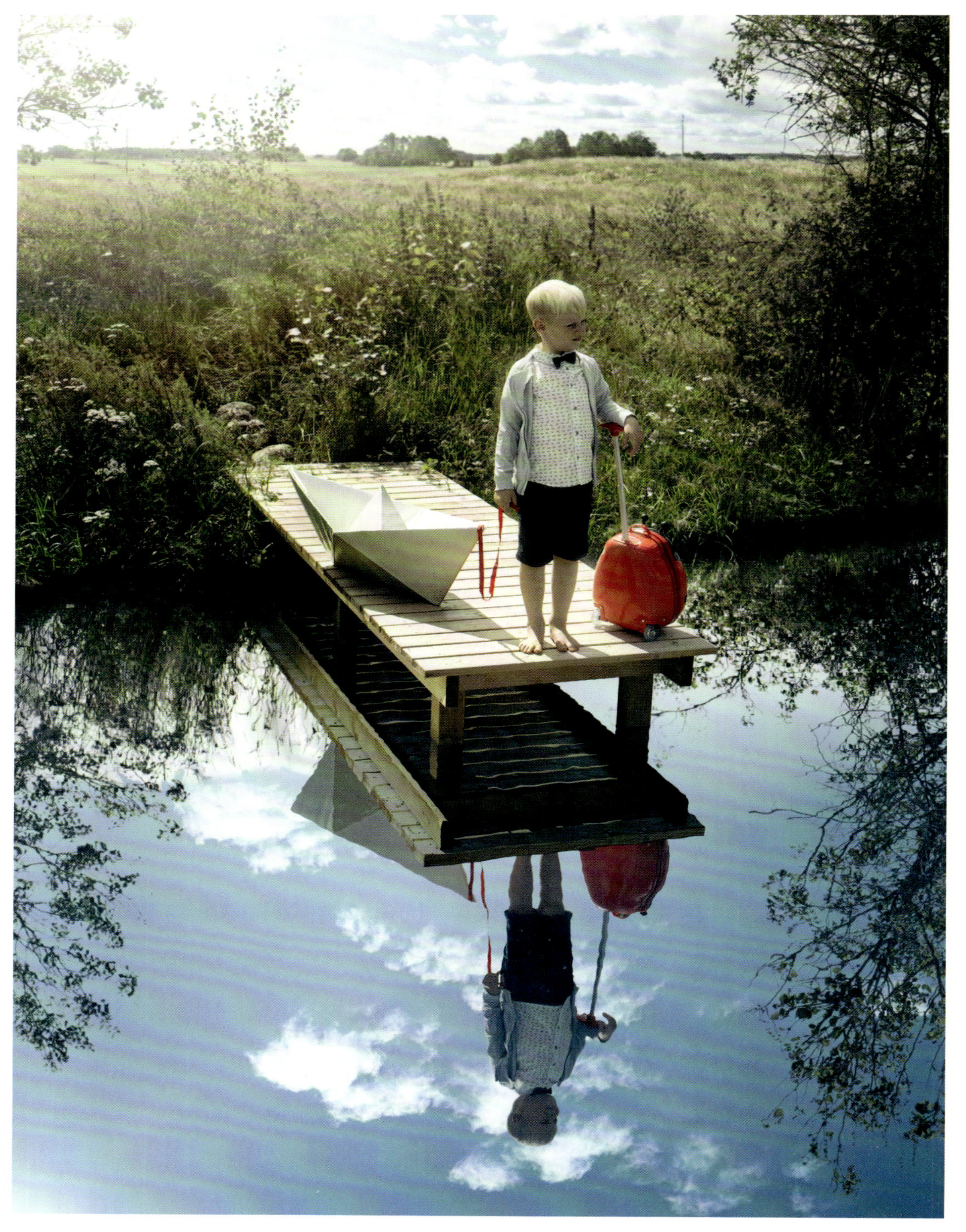

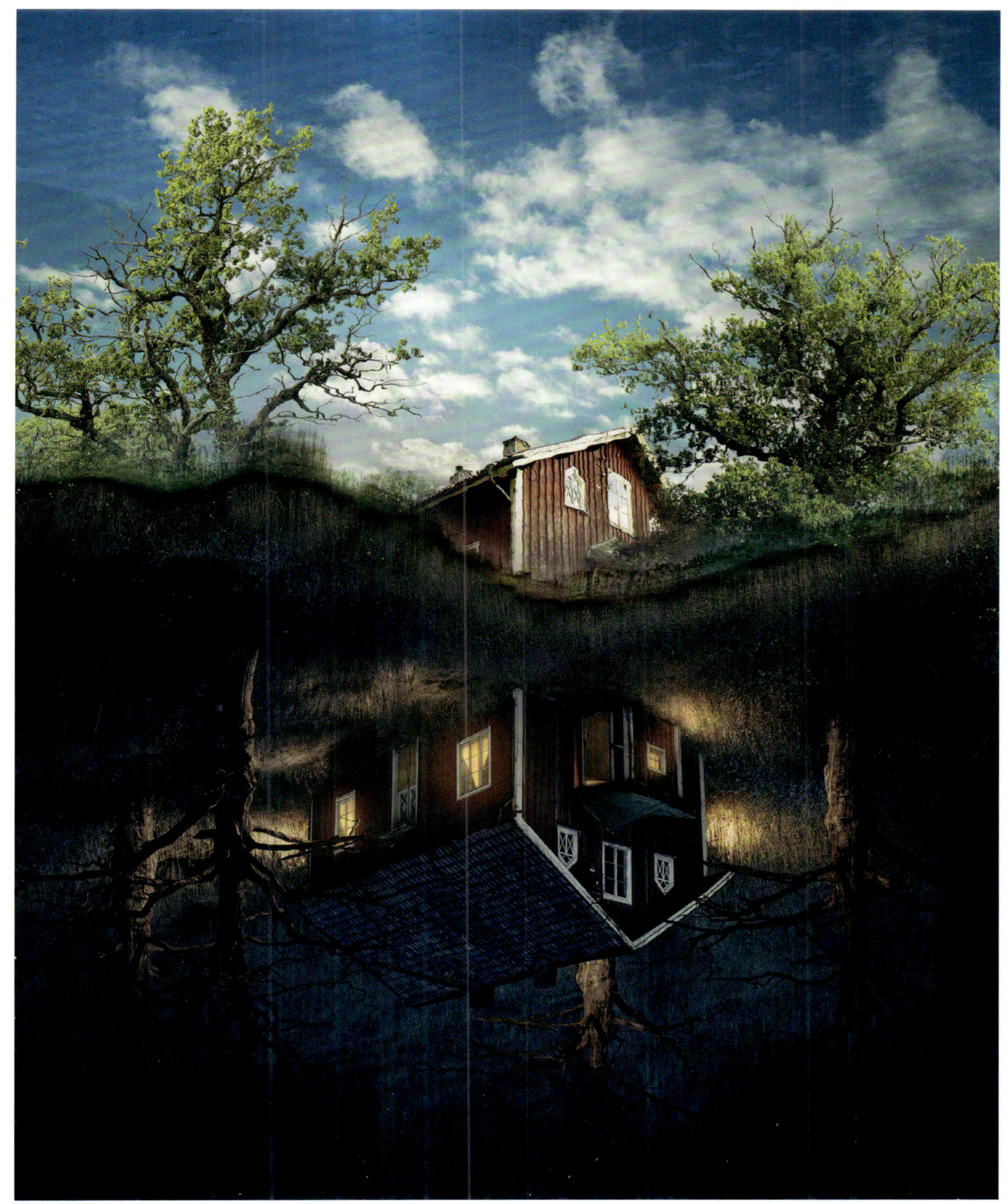

Burning Tree

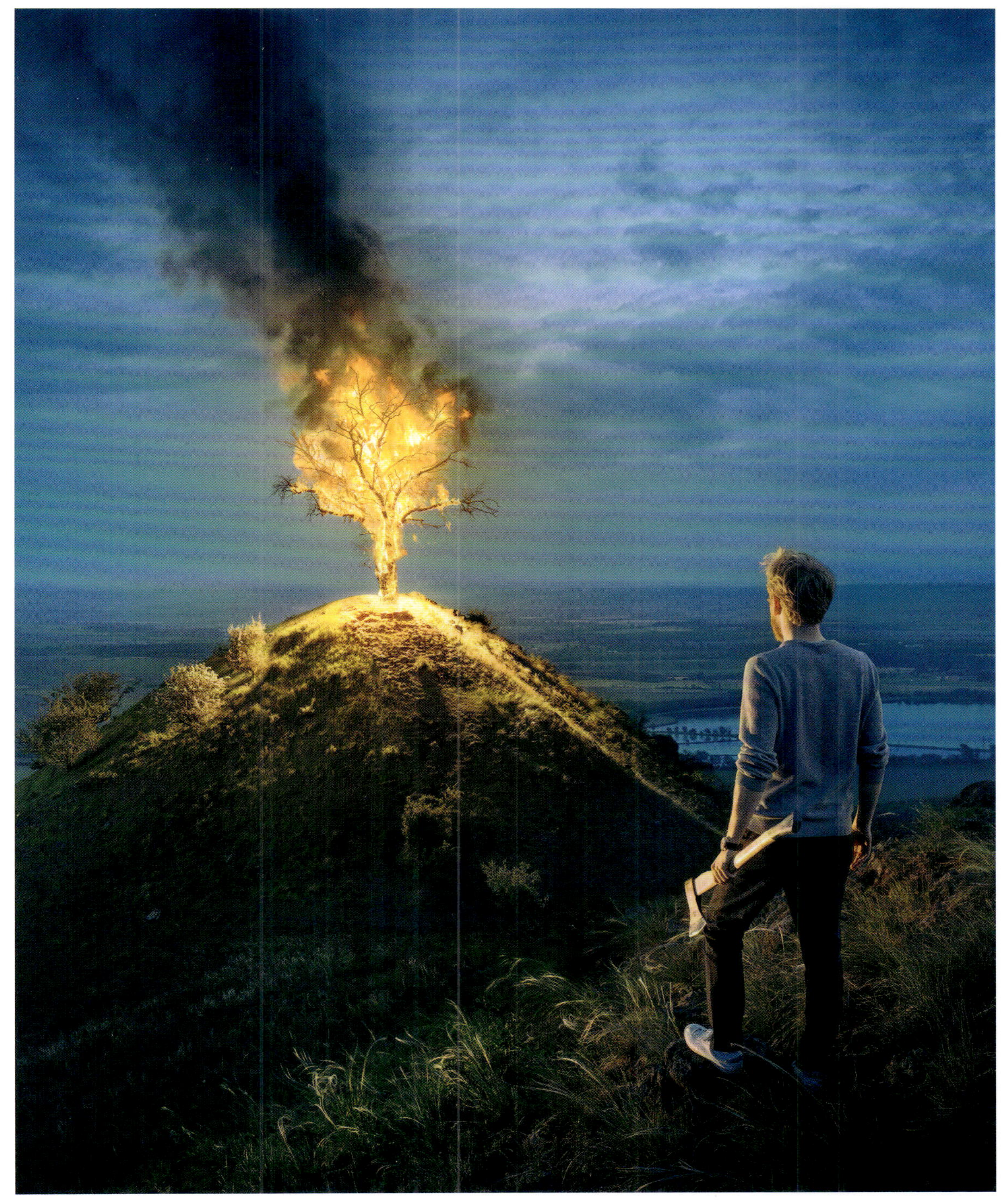

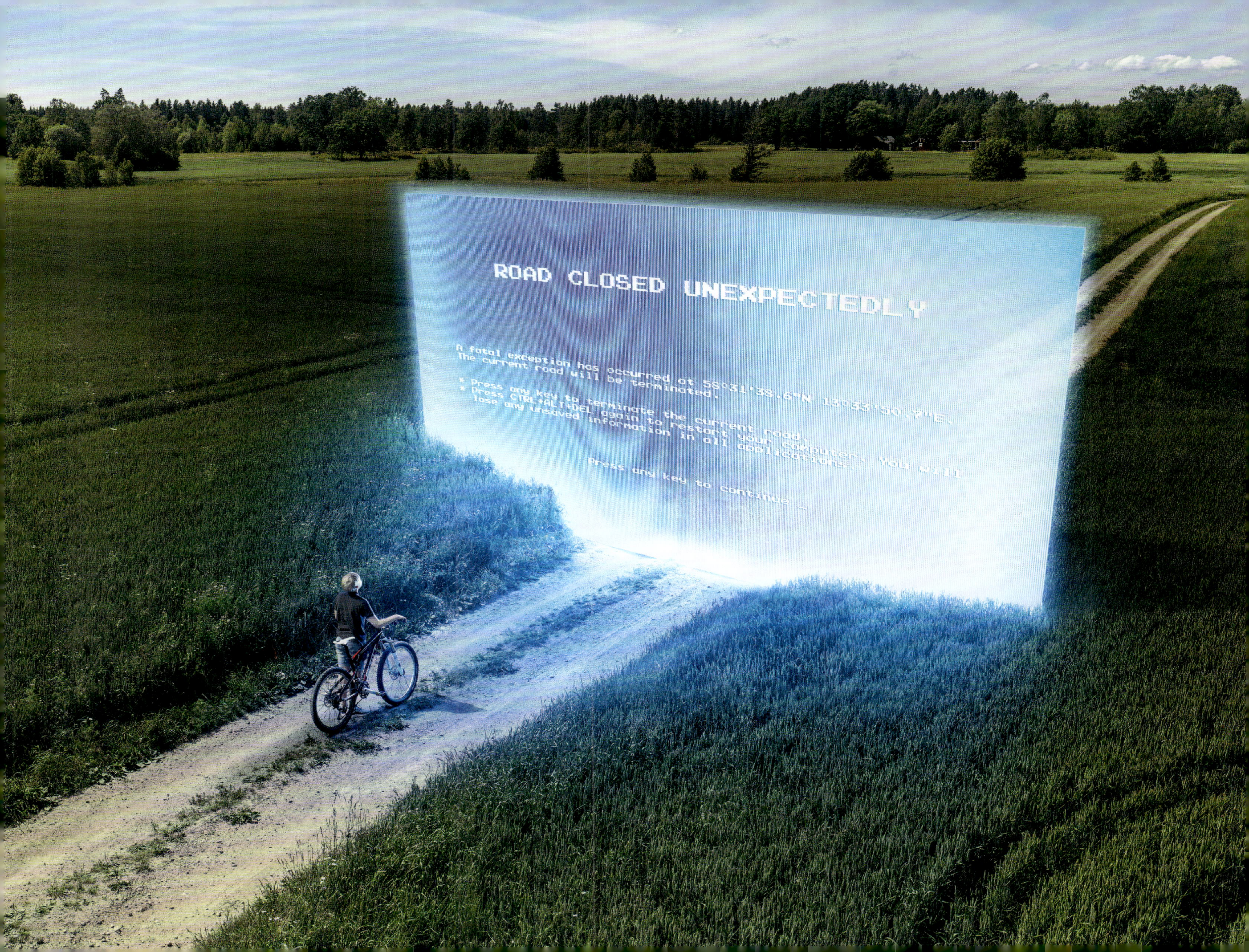

ROAD CLOSED UNEXPECTEDLY

A fatal exception has occurred at 58°31'33.6"N 13°33'50.7"E.
The current road will be terminated.

* Press any key to terminate the current road.
* Press CTRL+ALT+DEL again to restart your computer. You will
  lose any unsaved information in all applications.

Press any key to continue _

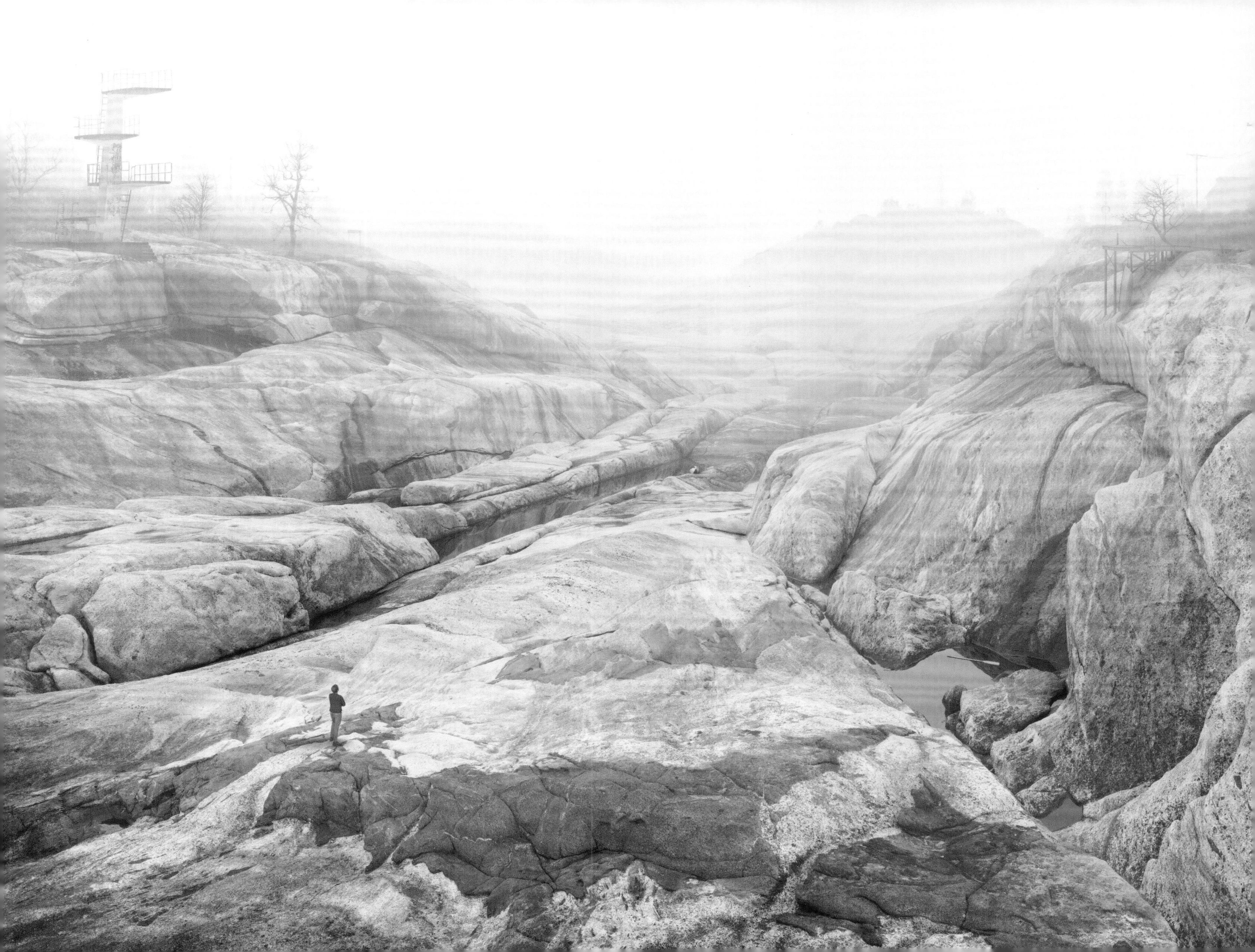

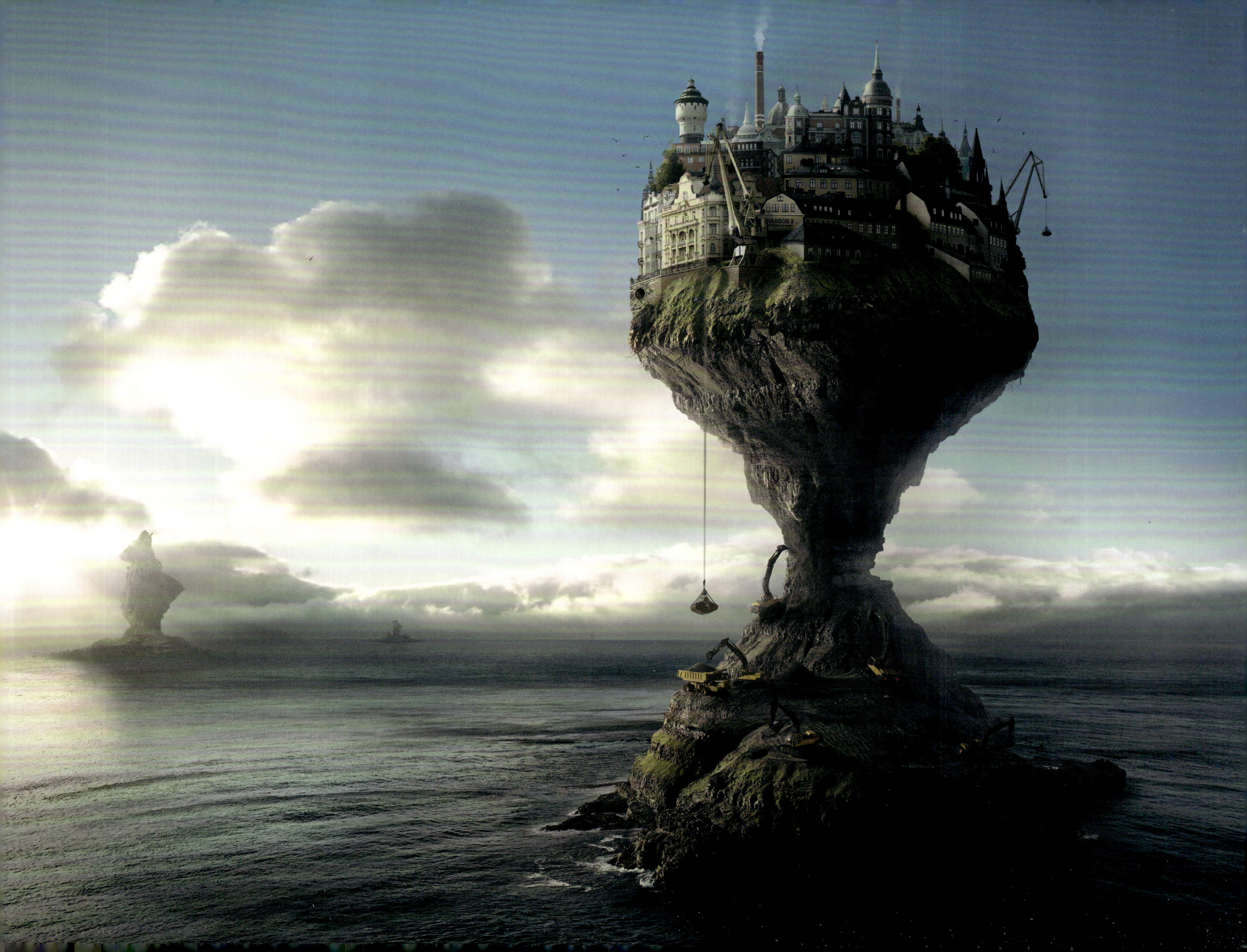
HARBOR 3

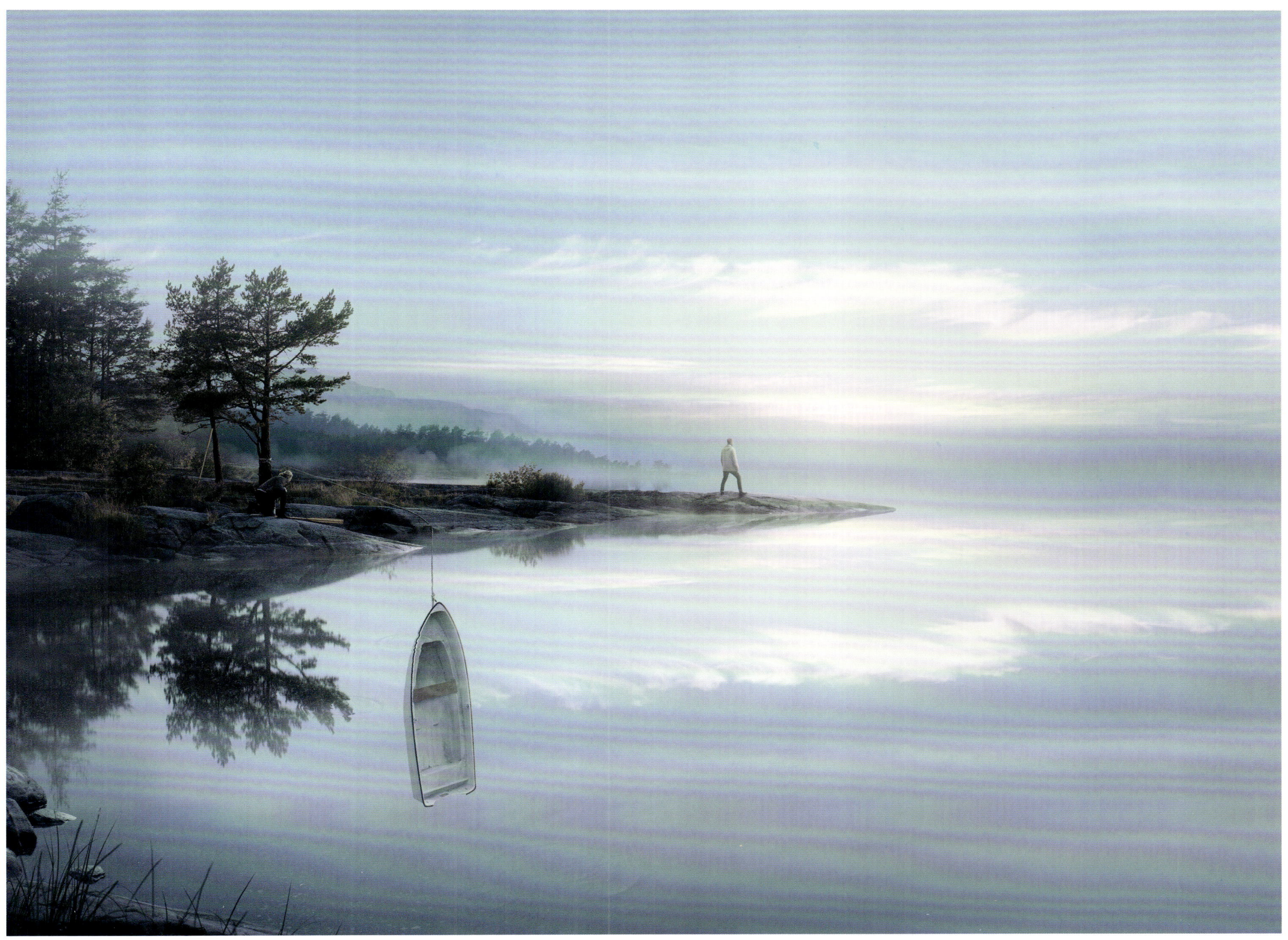

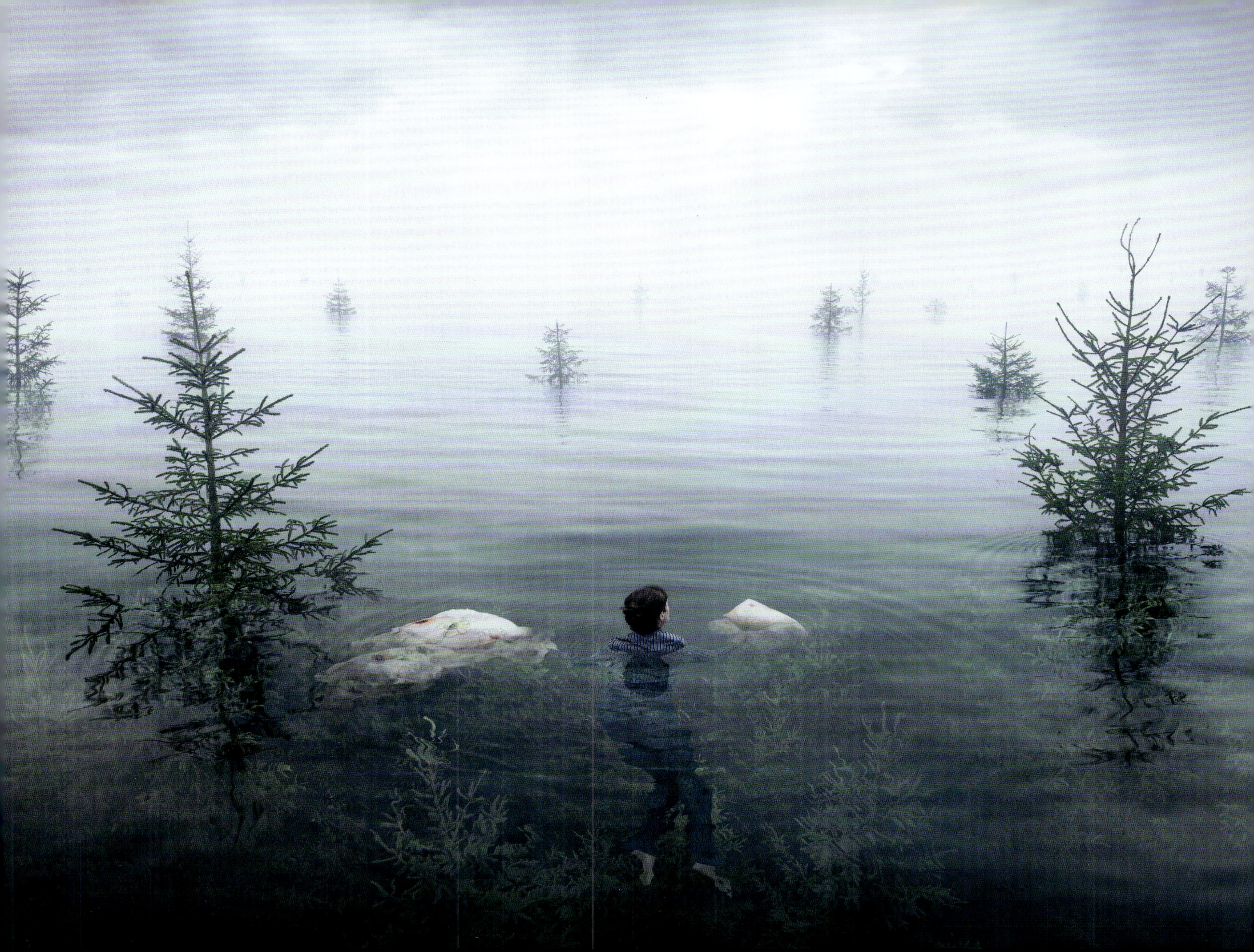

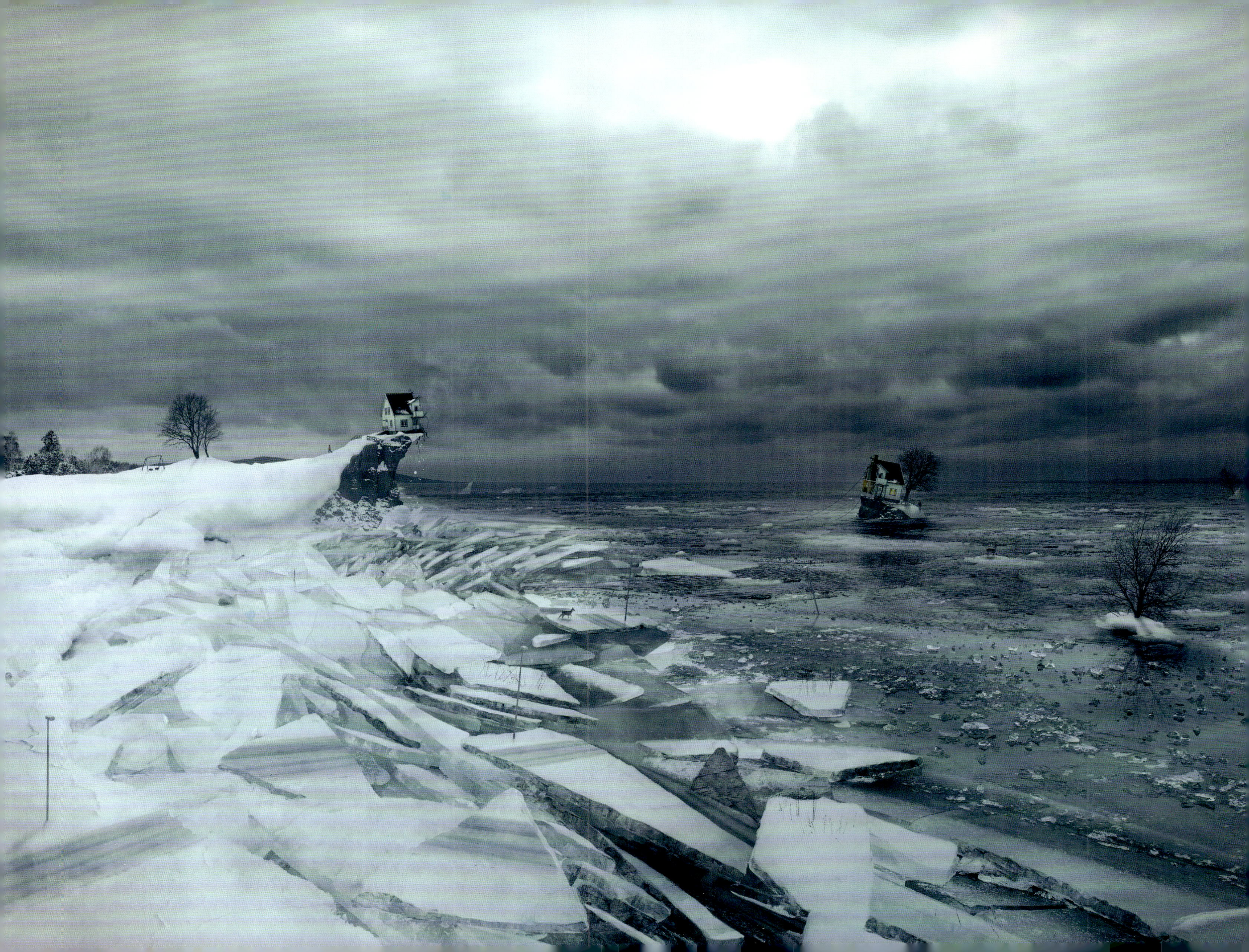

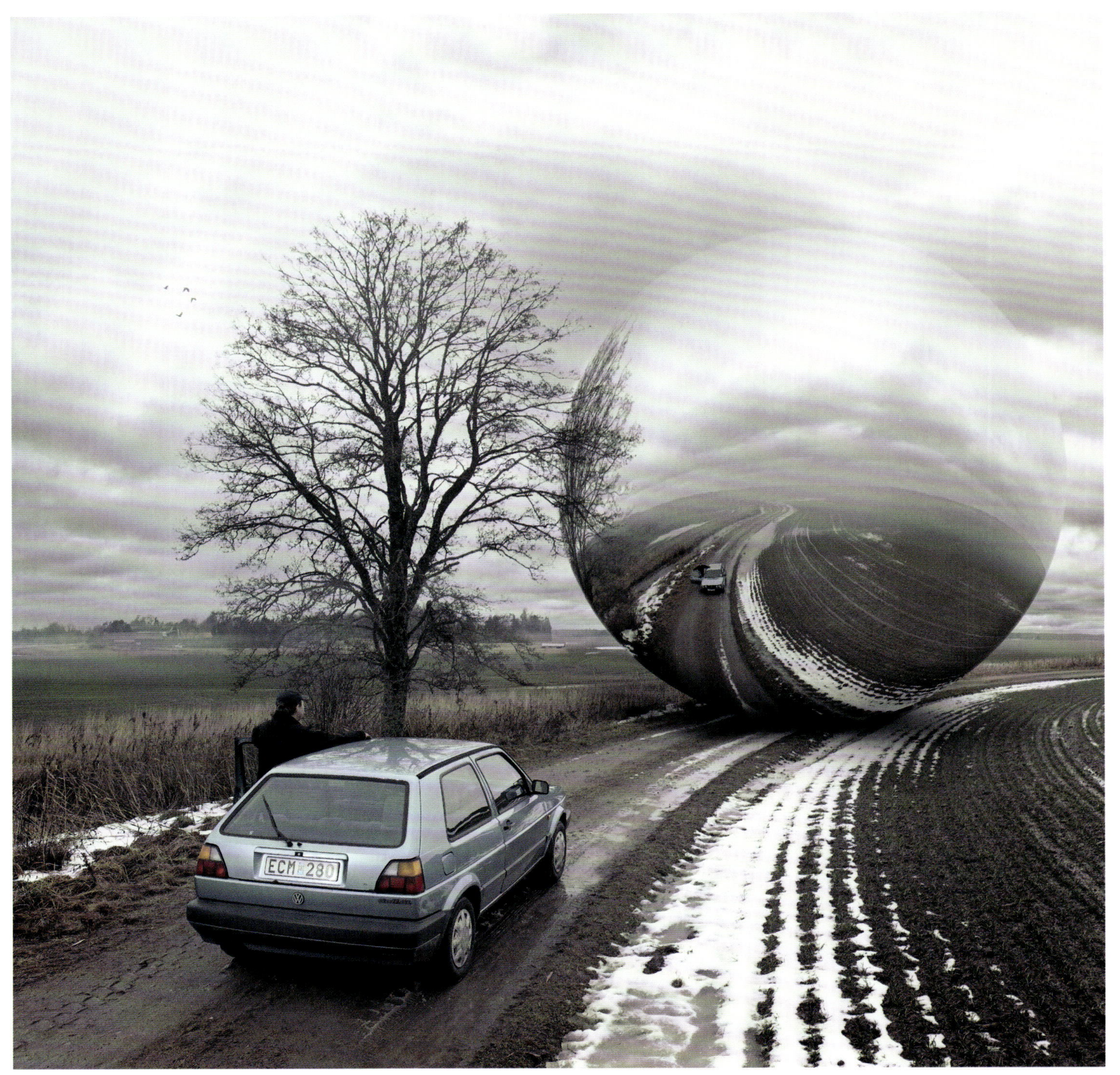

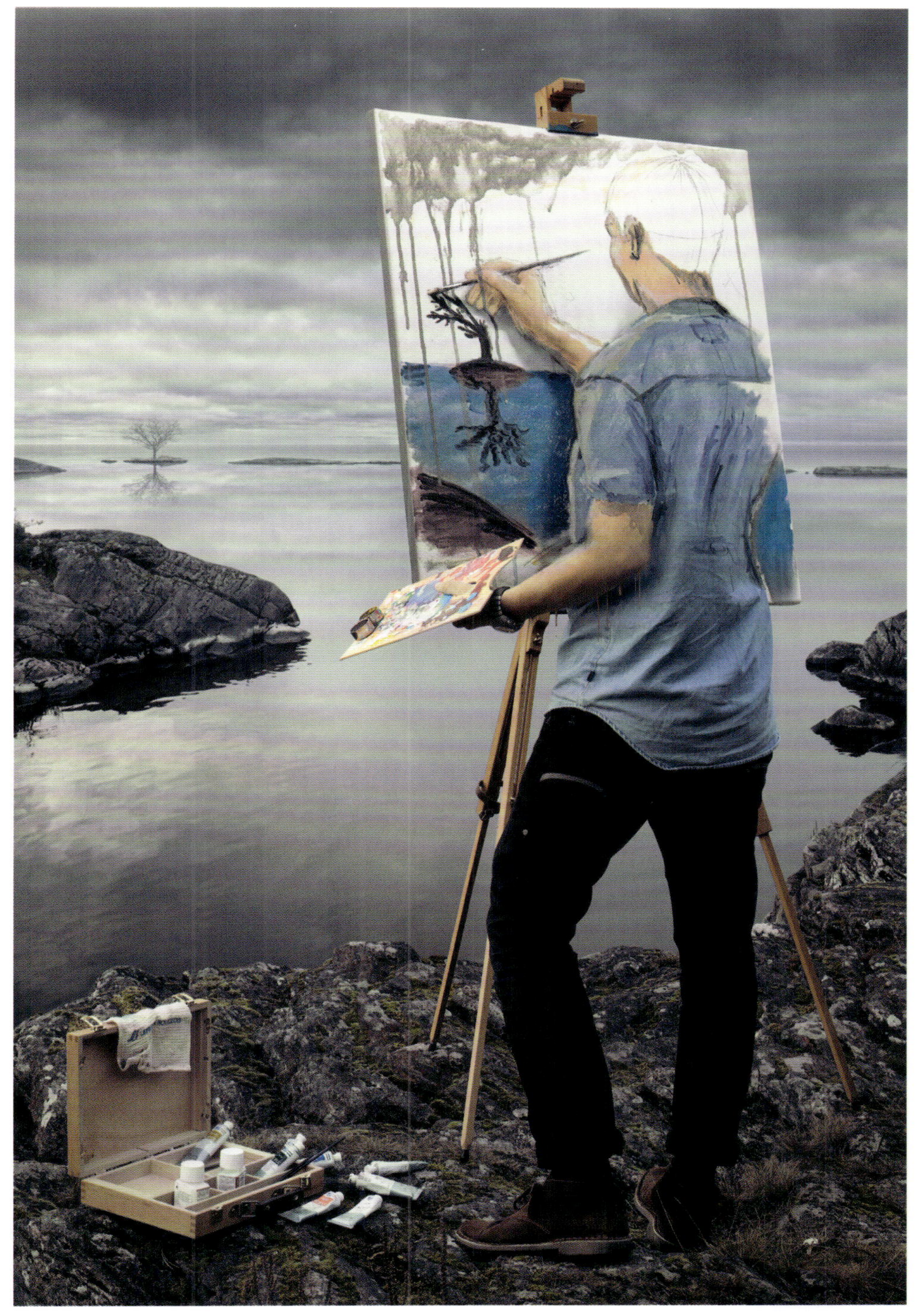

End of Line

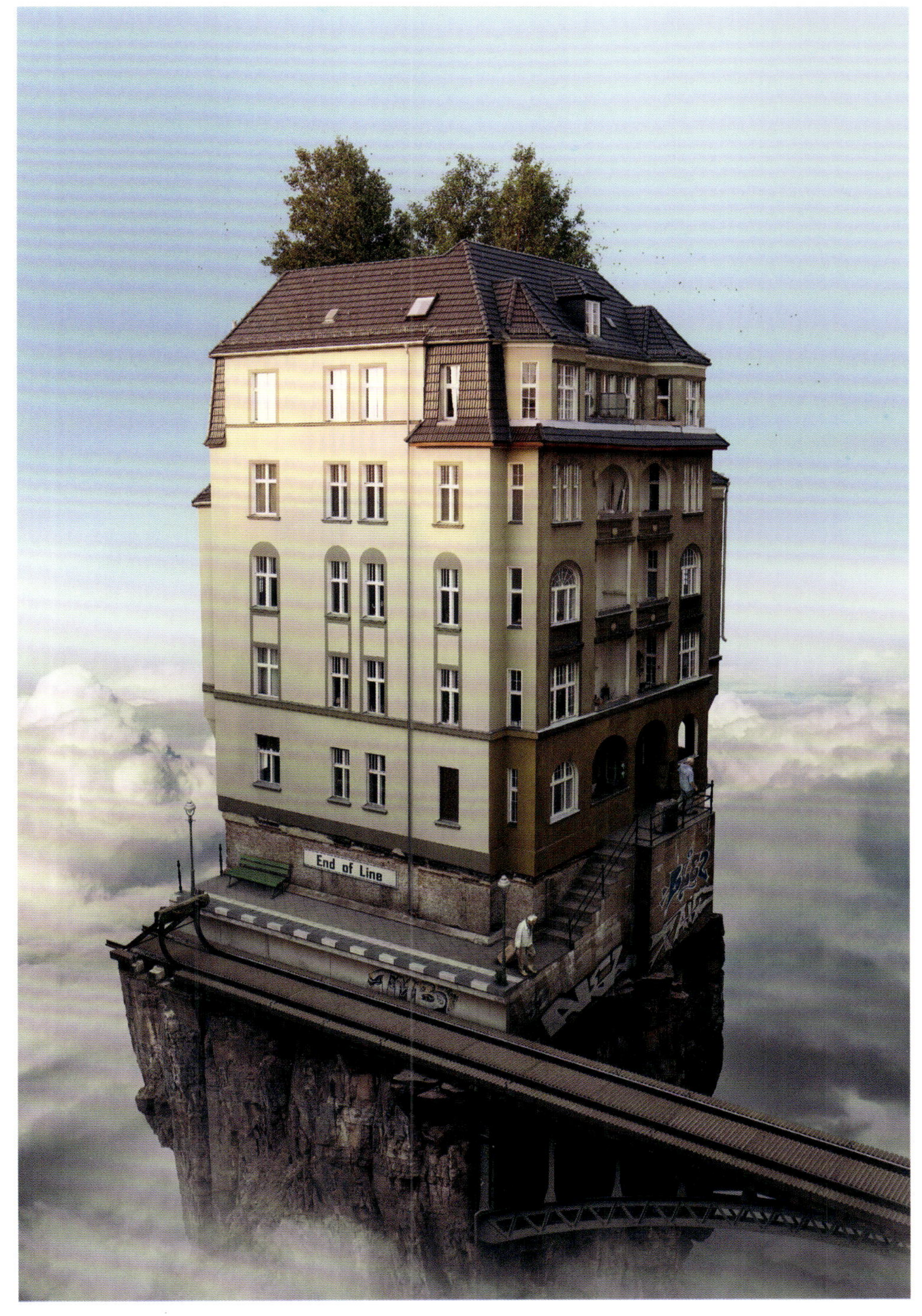
End of Line

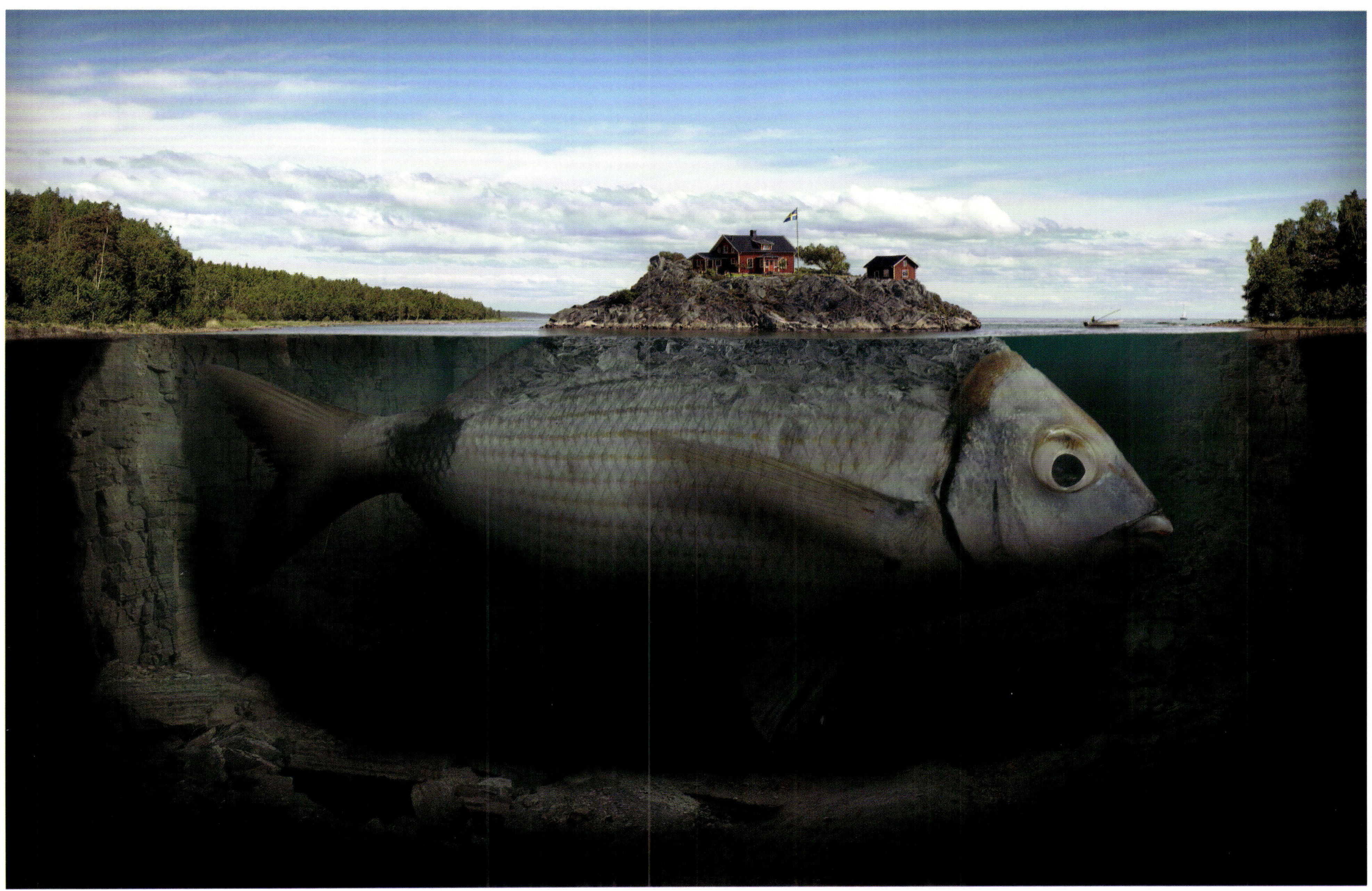

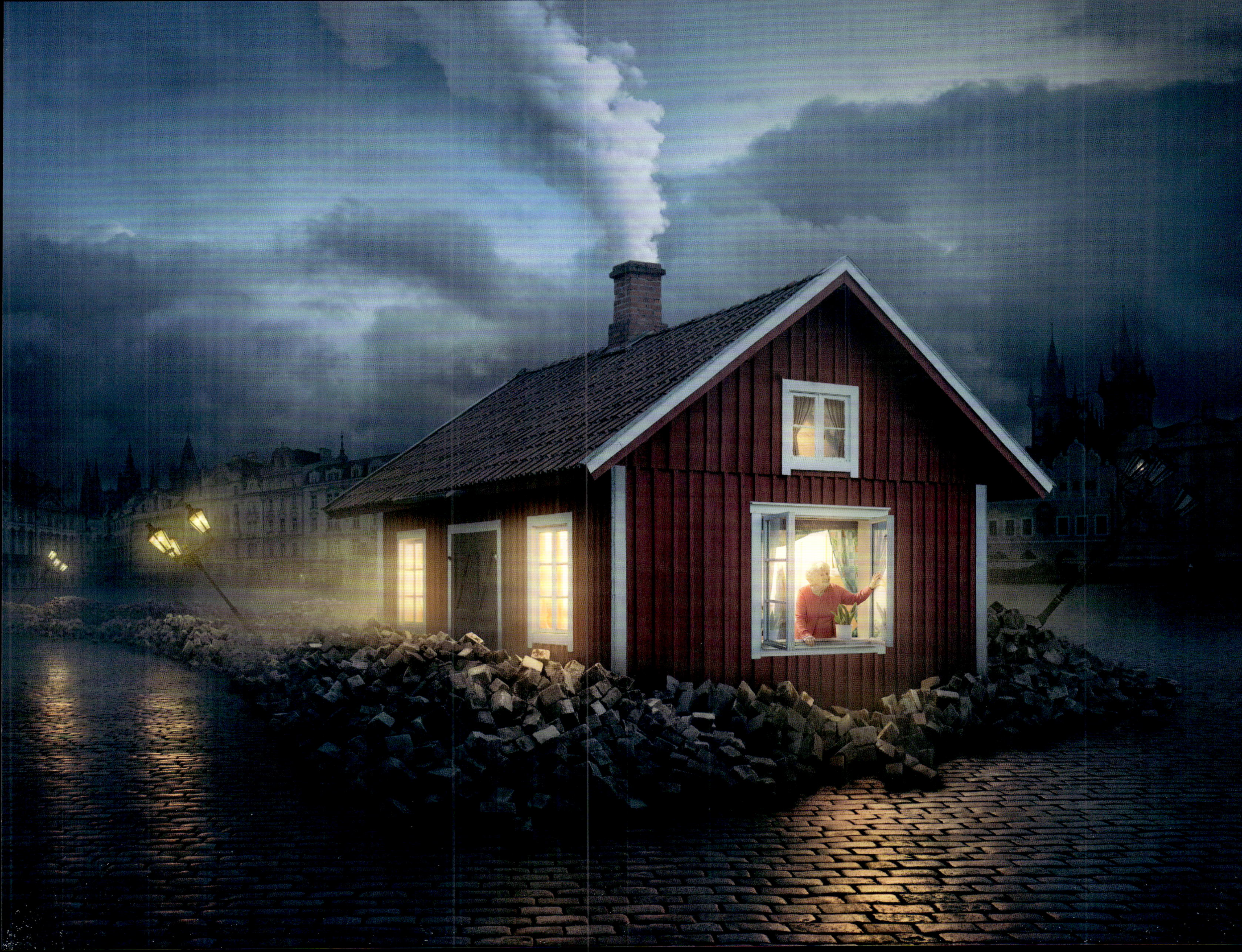

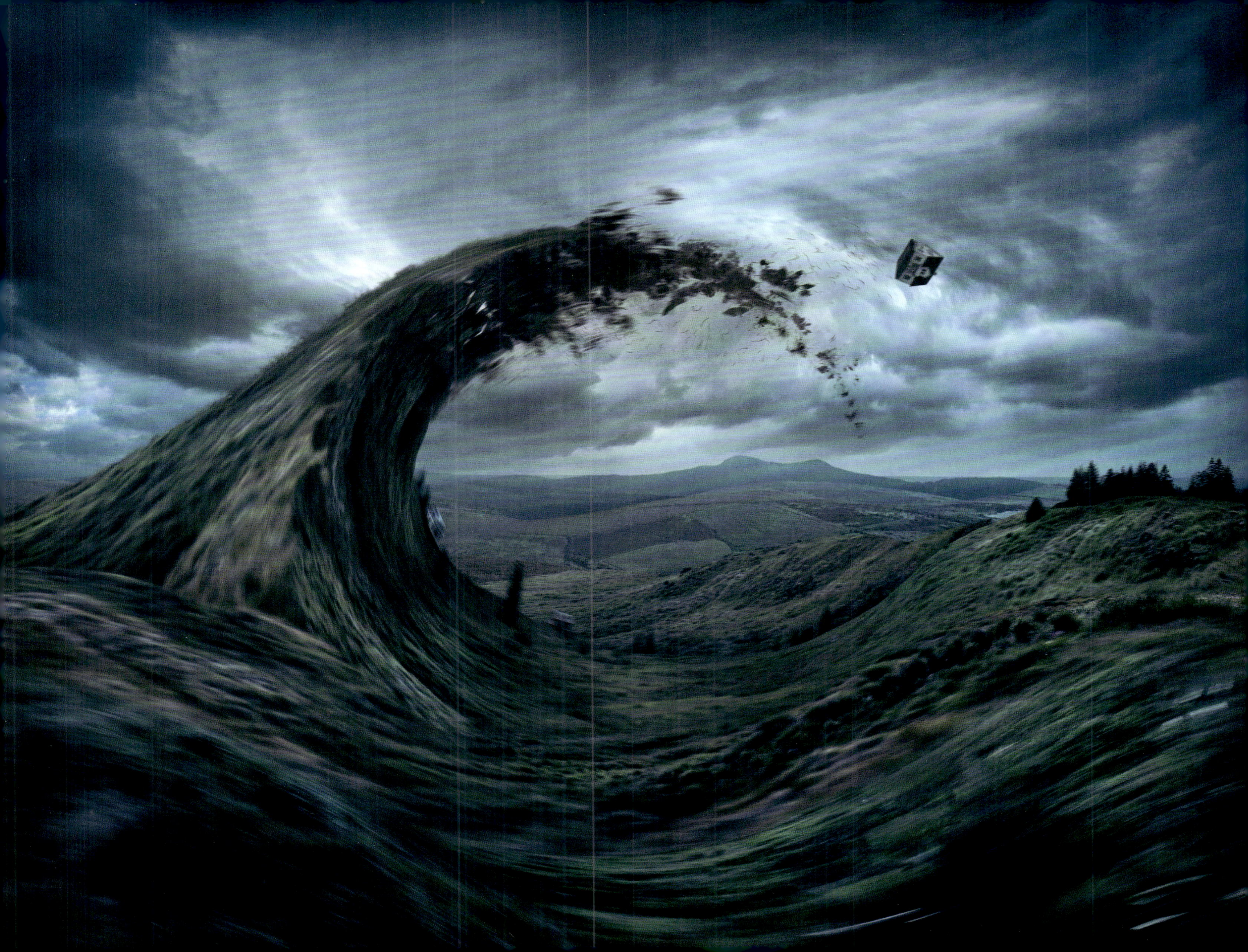

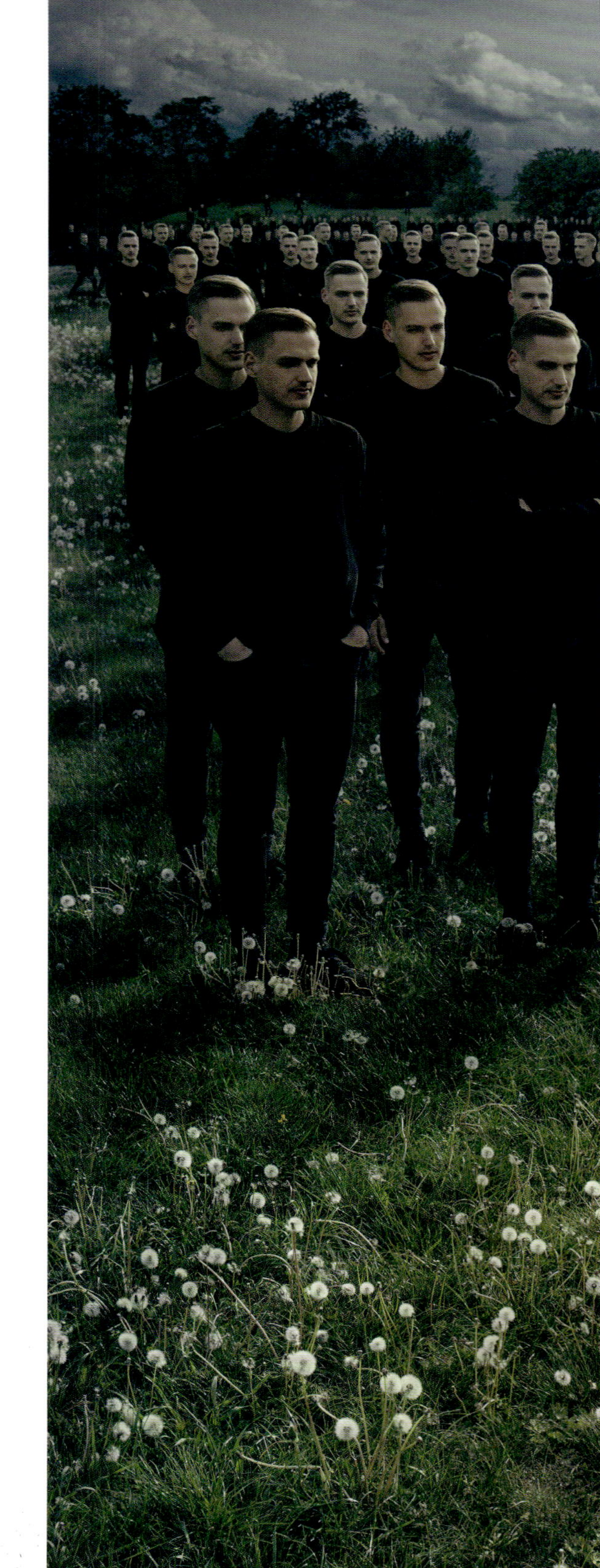

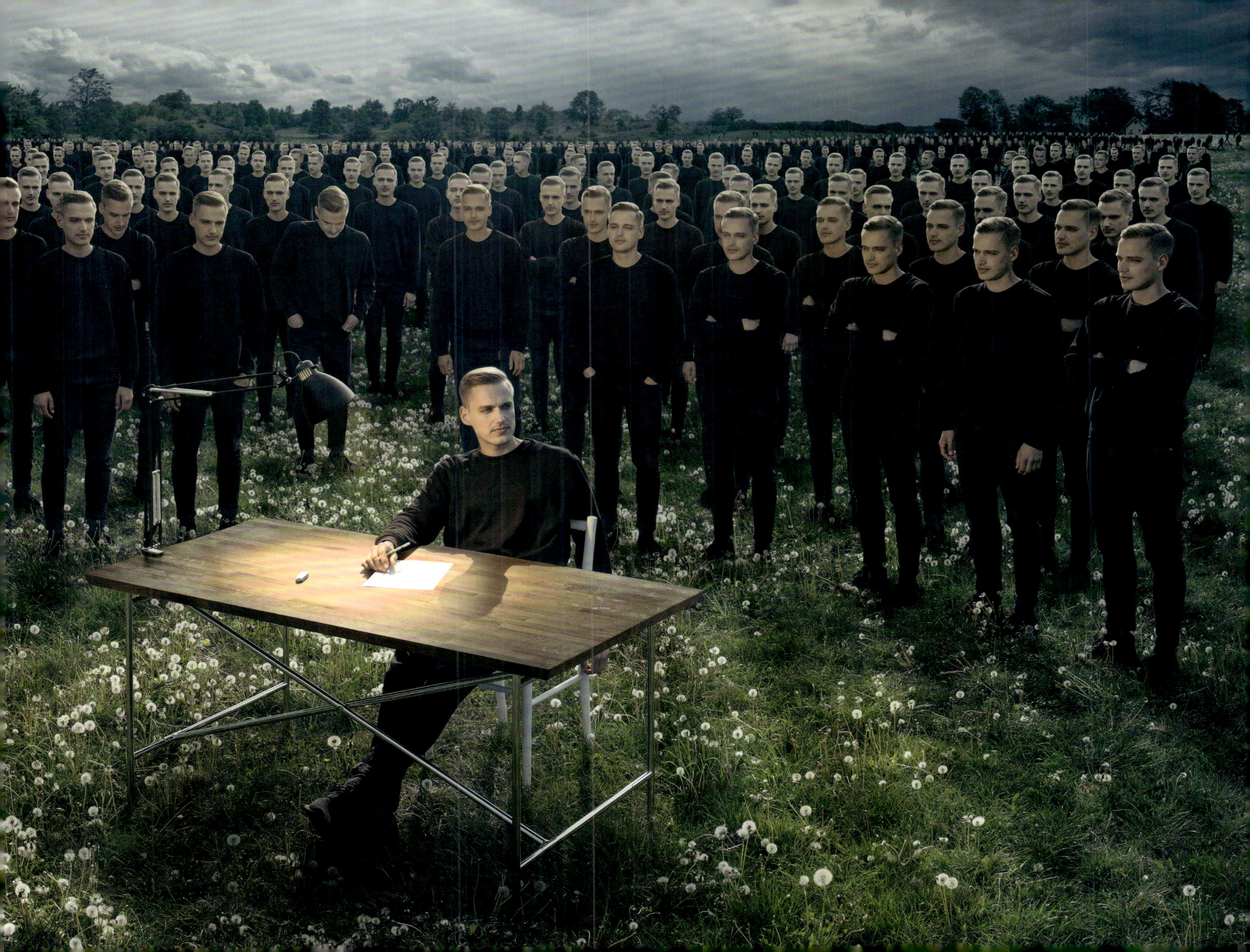

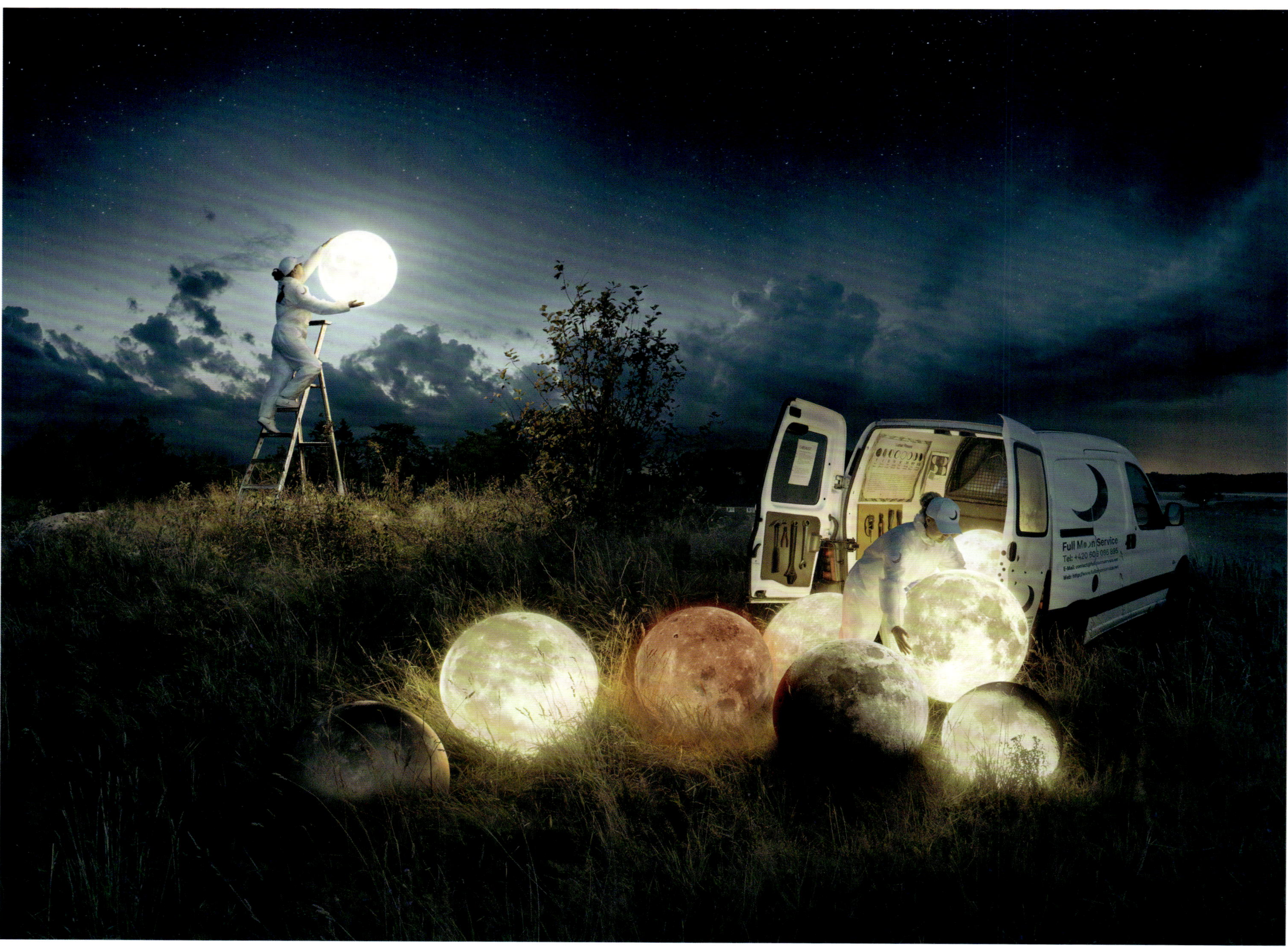

Full Moon Service
Tel: +420 603 095 895
E-Mail: contact@fullmoonservice.net
Web: http://www.fullmoonservice.net

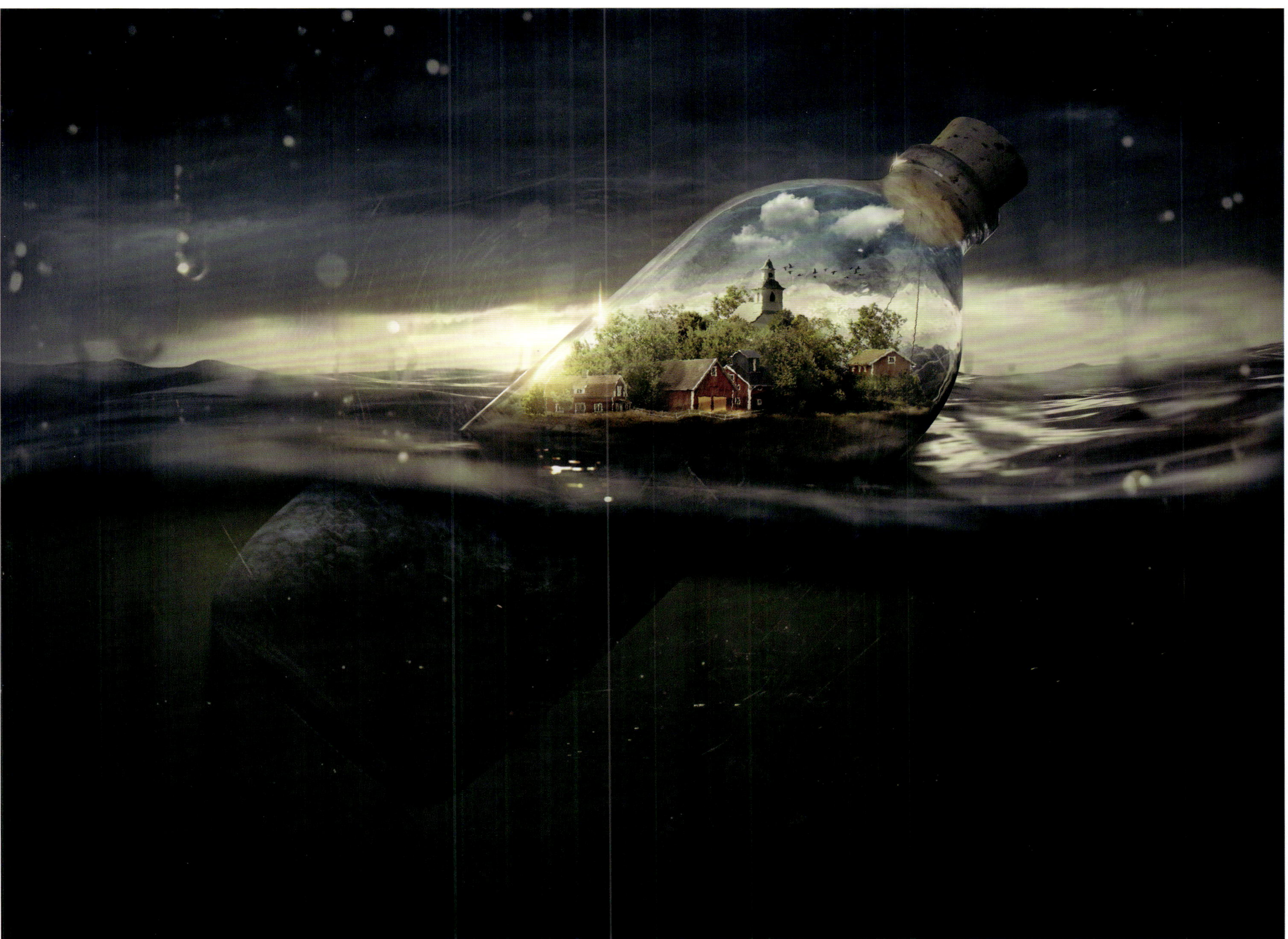

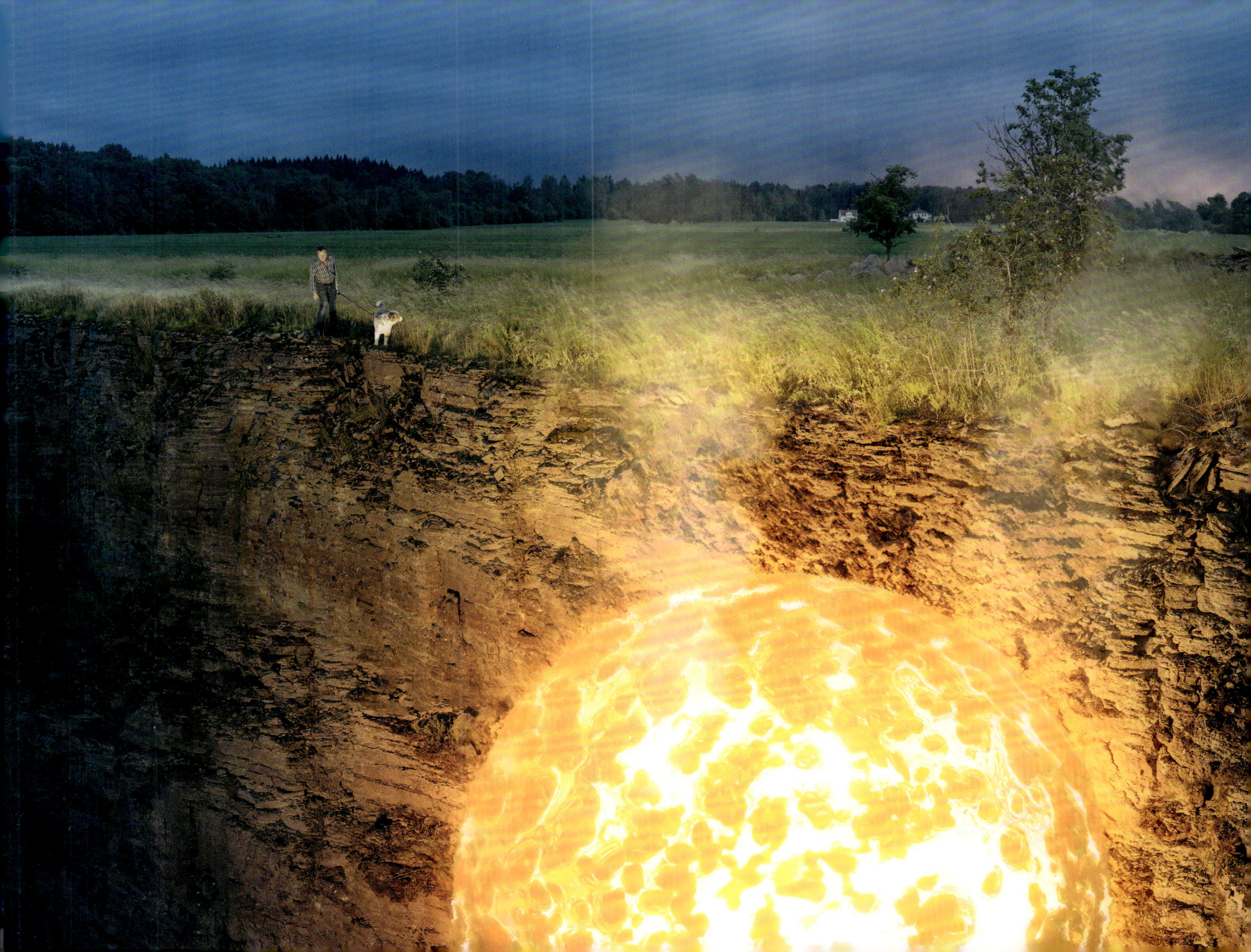

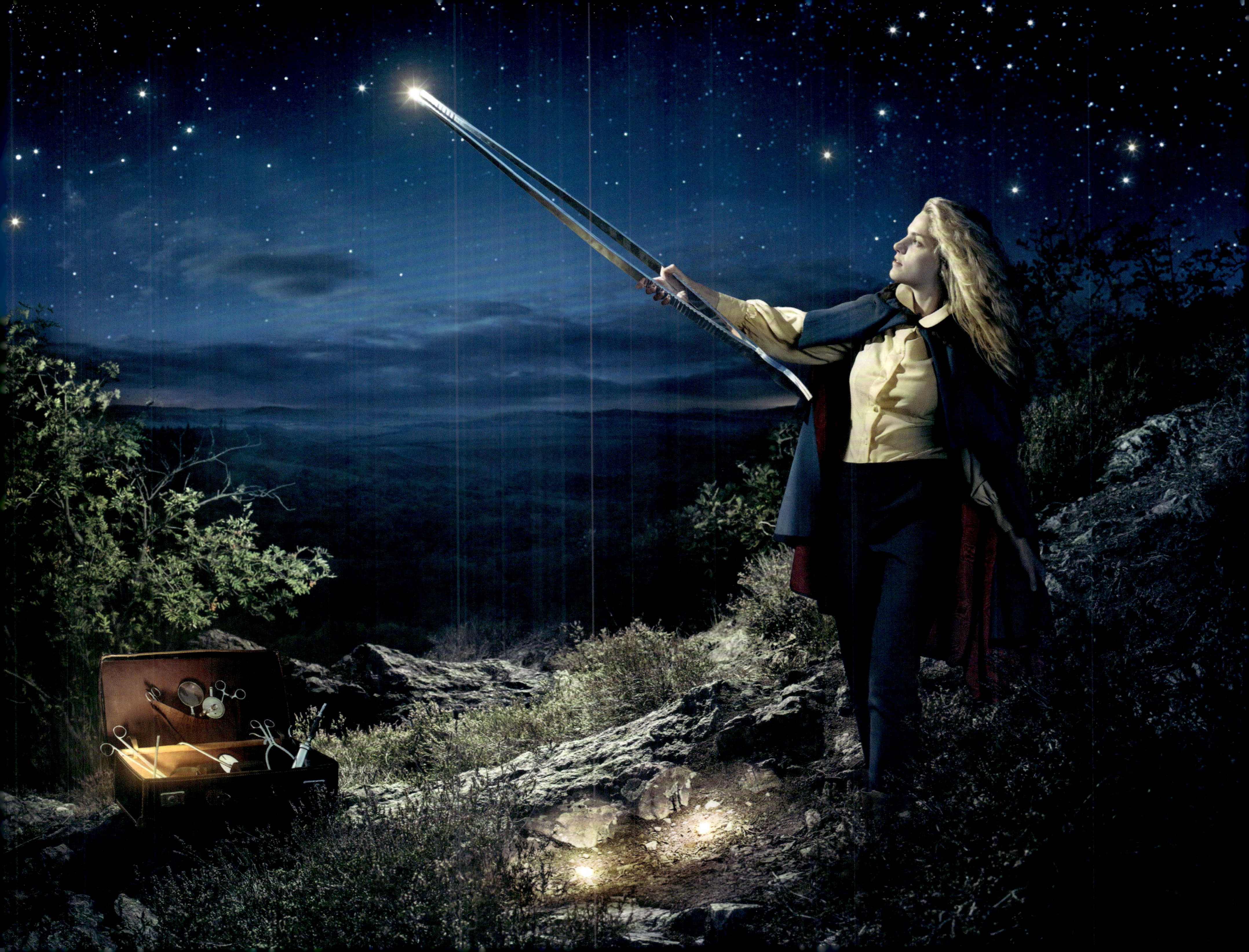

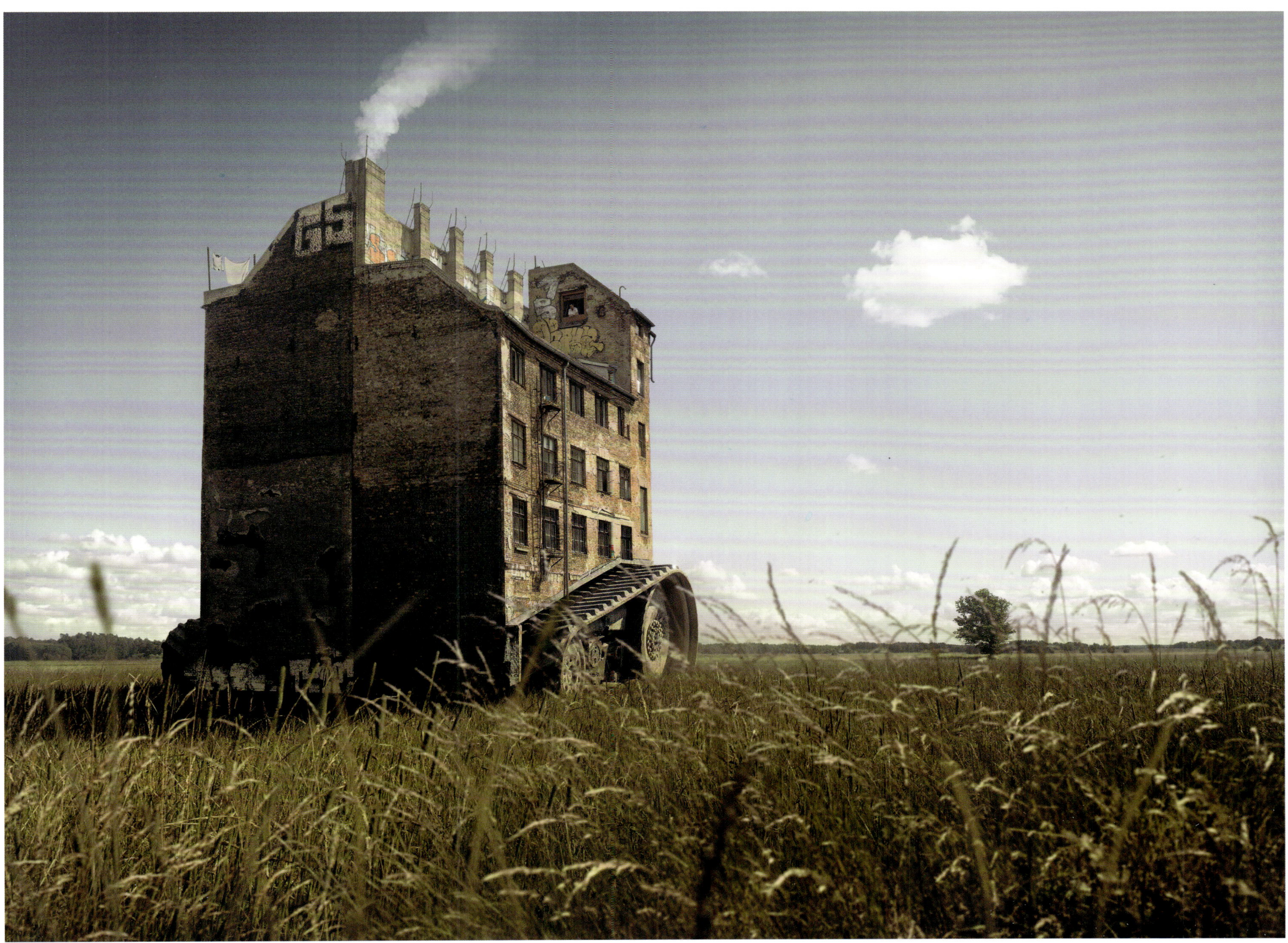

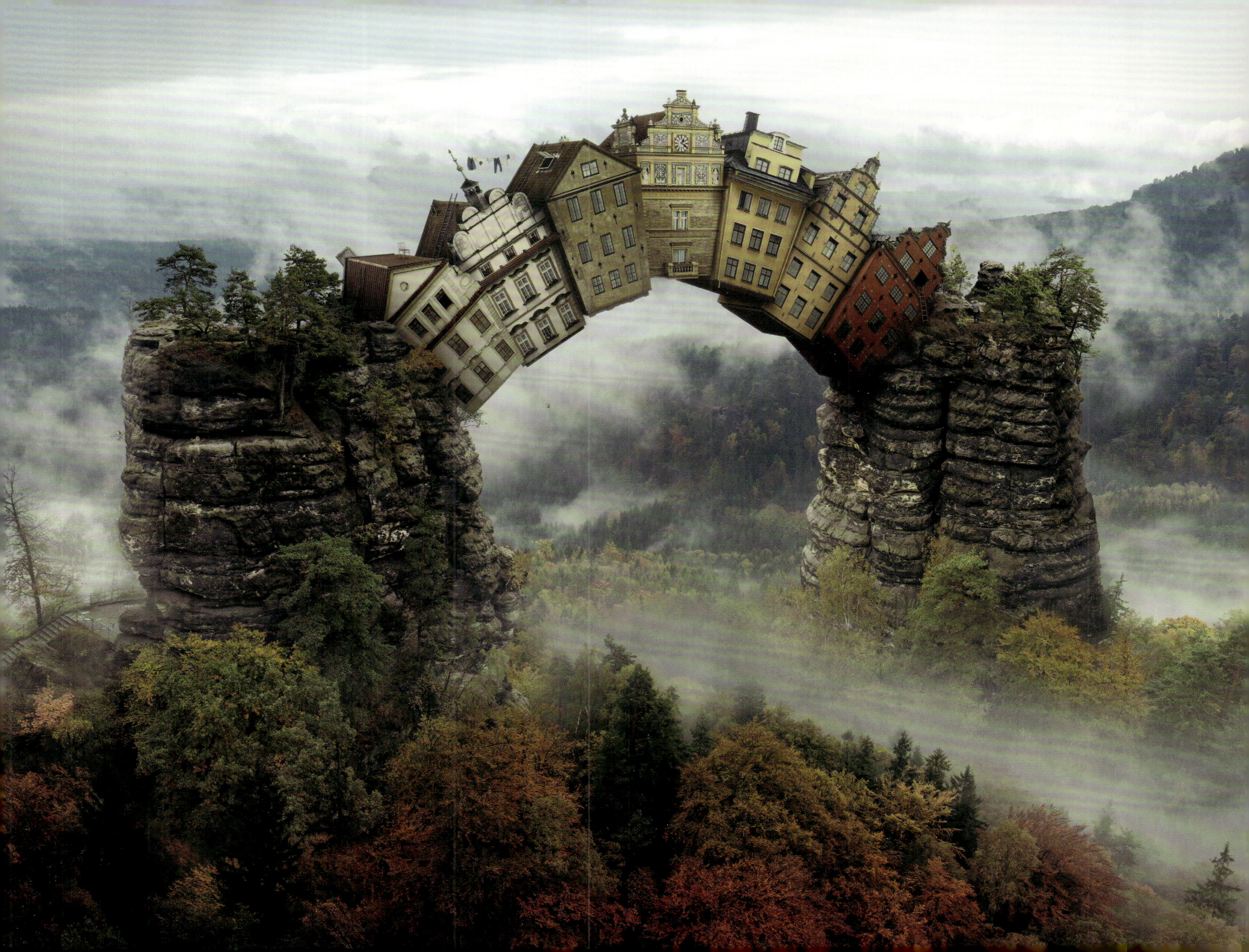

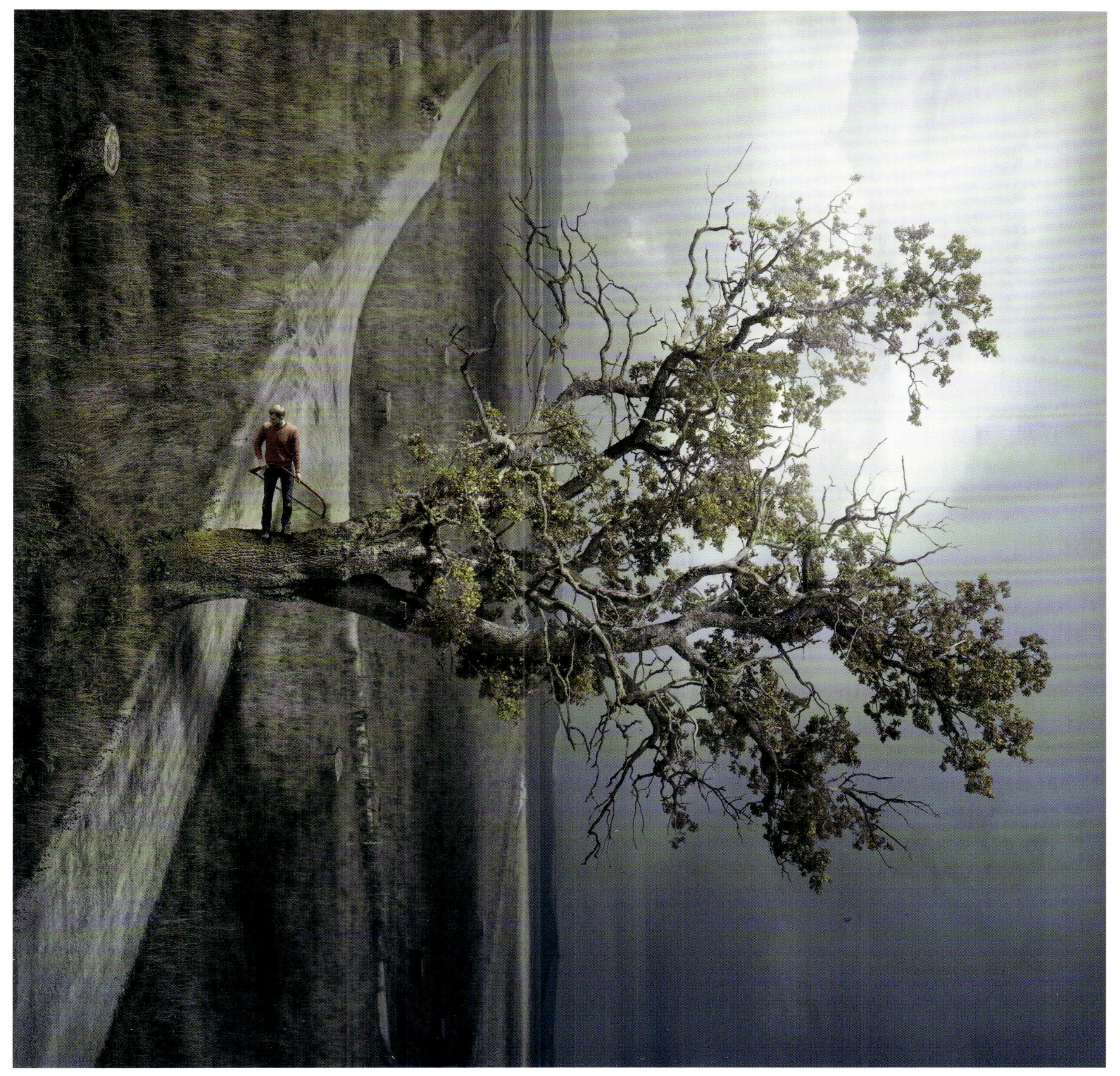

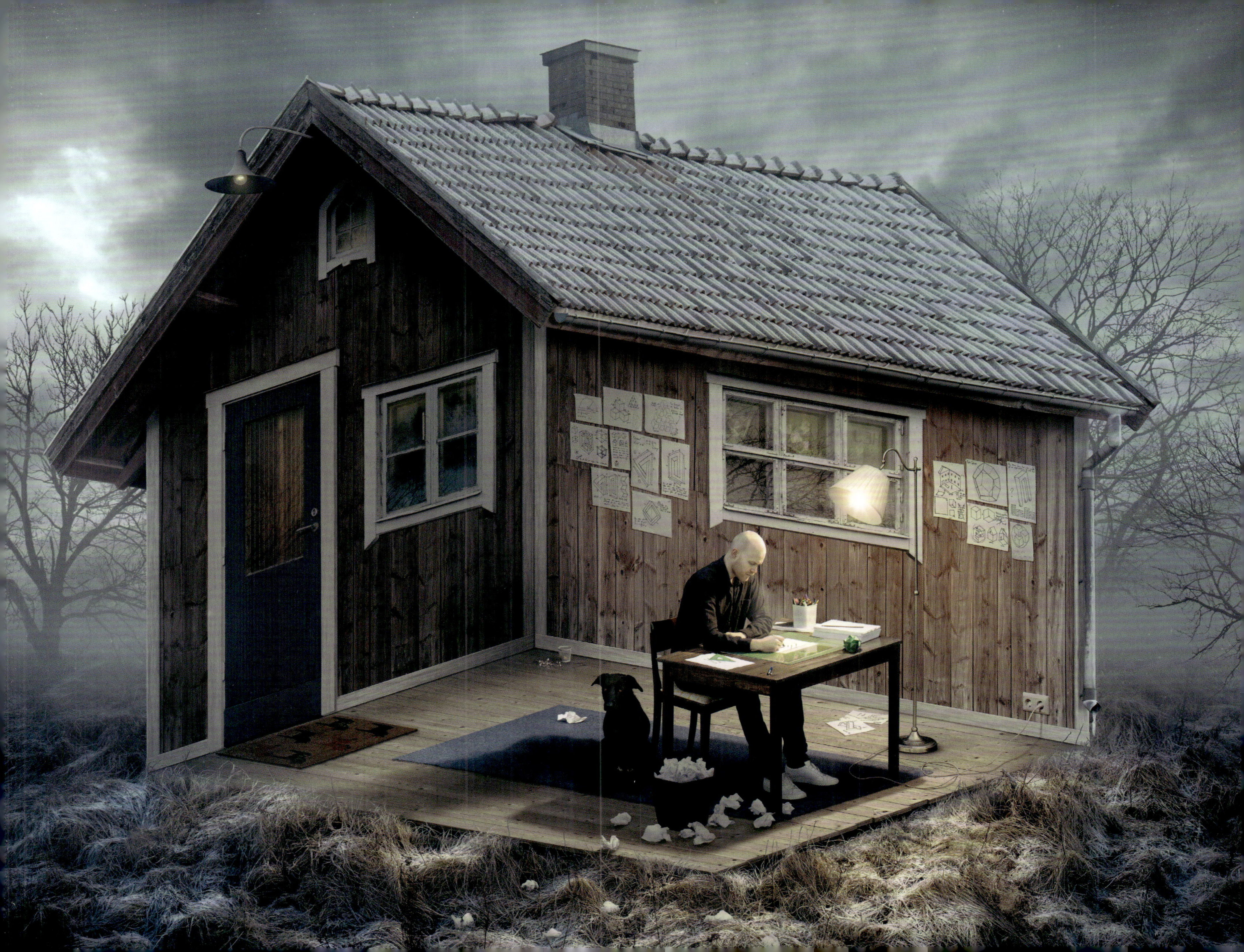

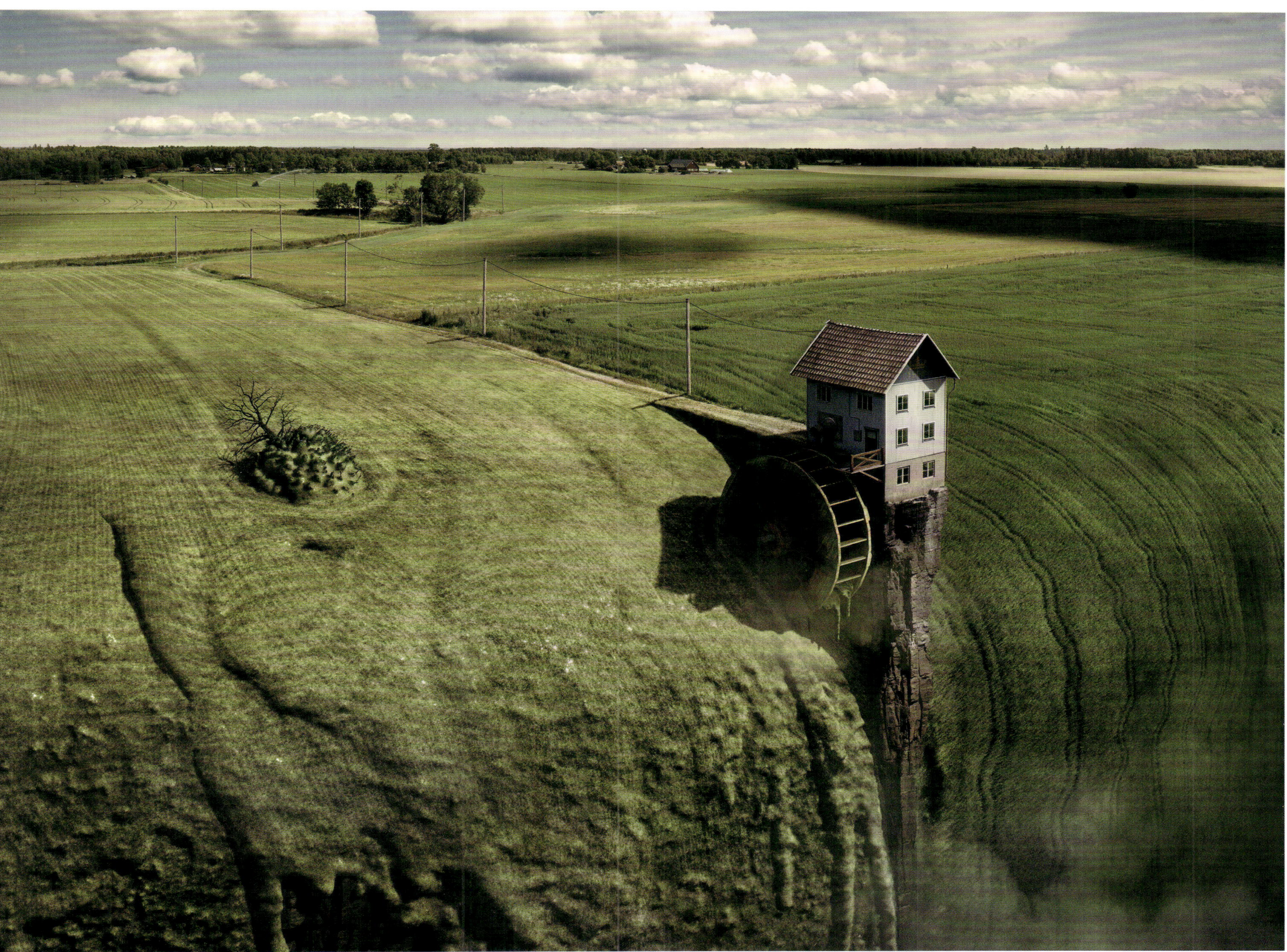

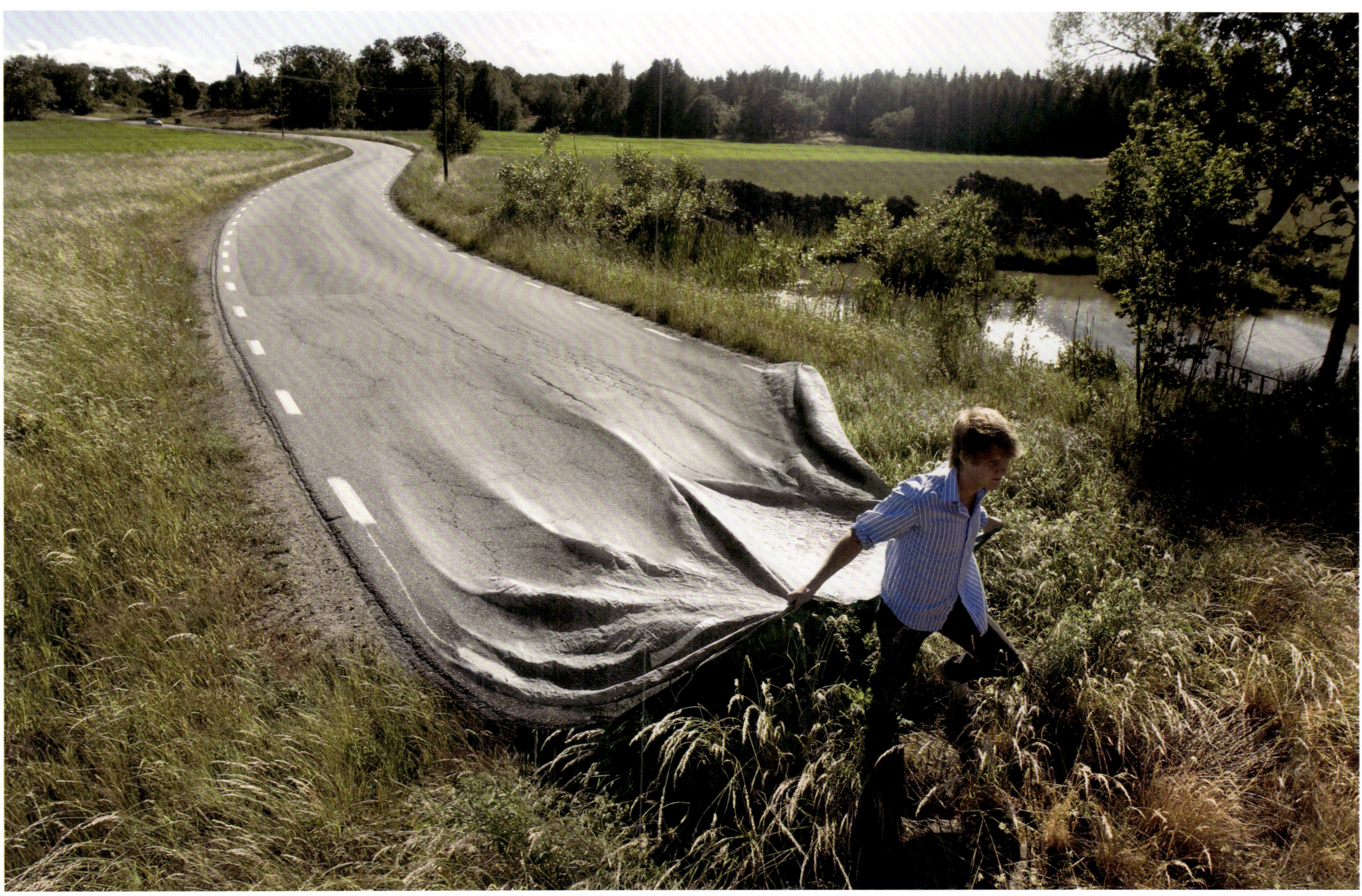

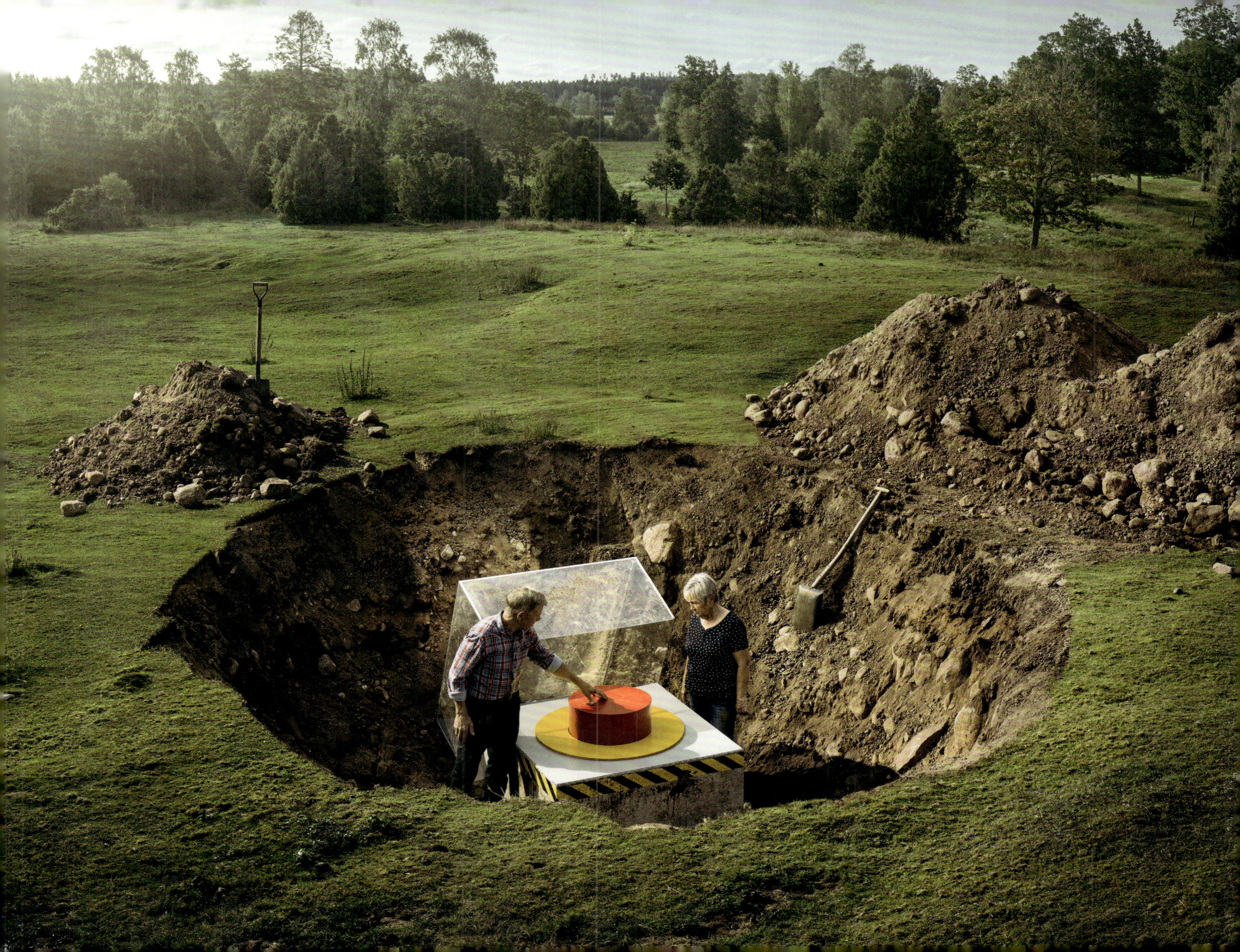

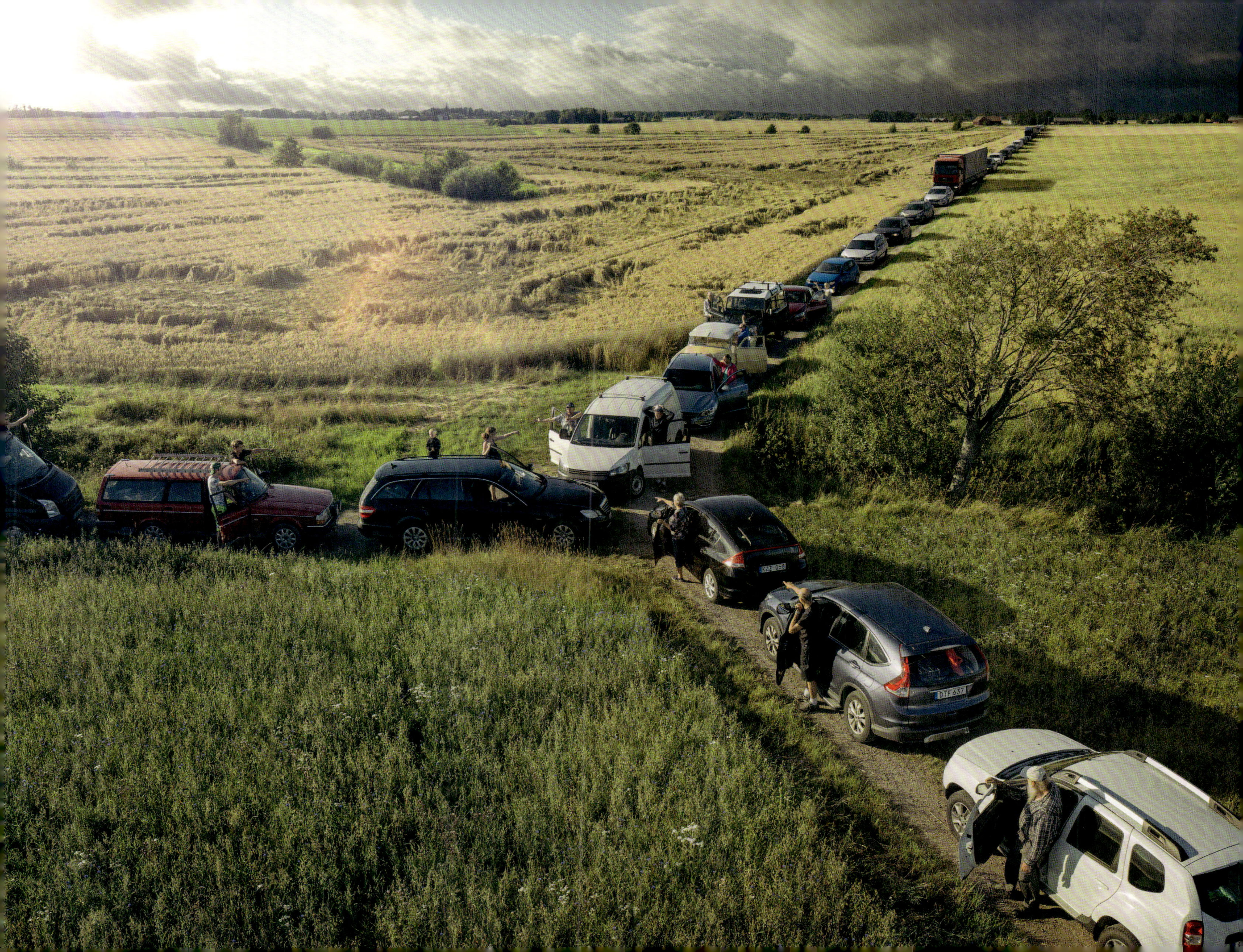

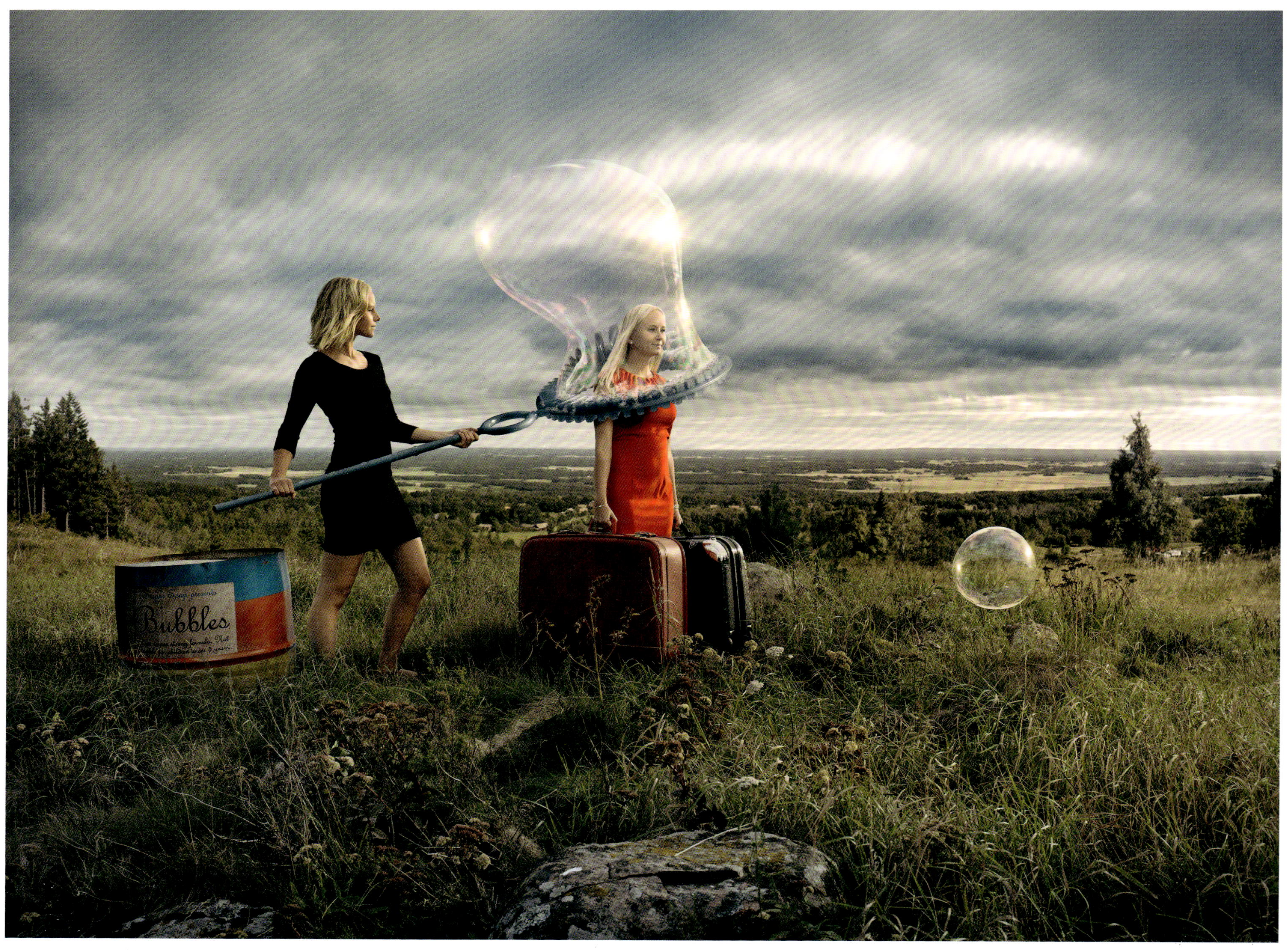
Super Soap presents
Bubbles
extra strong formula. Not
for children under 5 years!

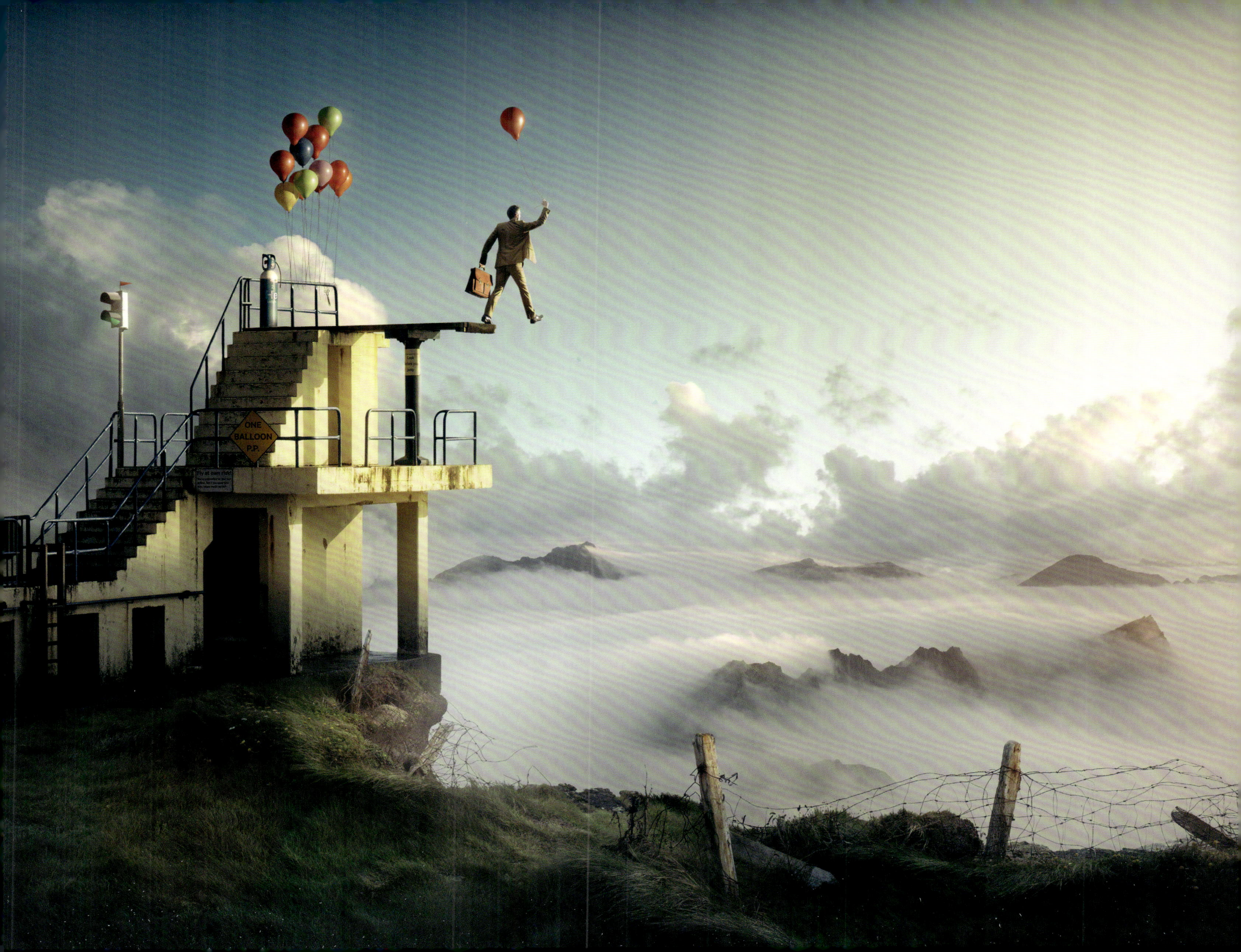

ONE
BALLOON
P.P.

Fly at own risk!

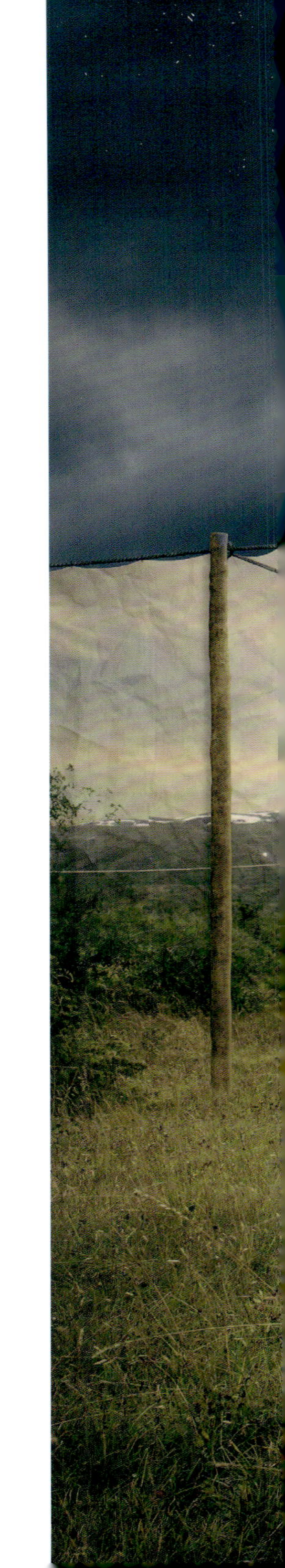

The Cover-Up

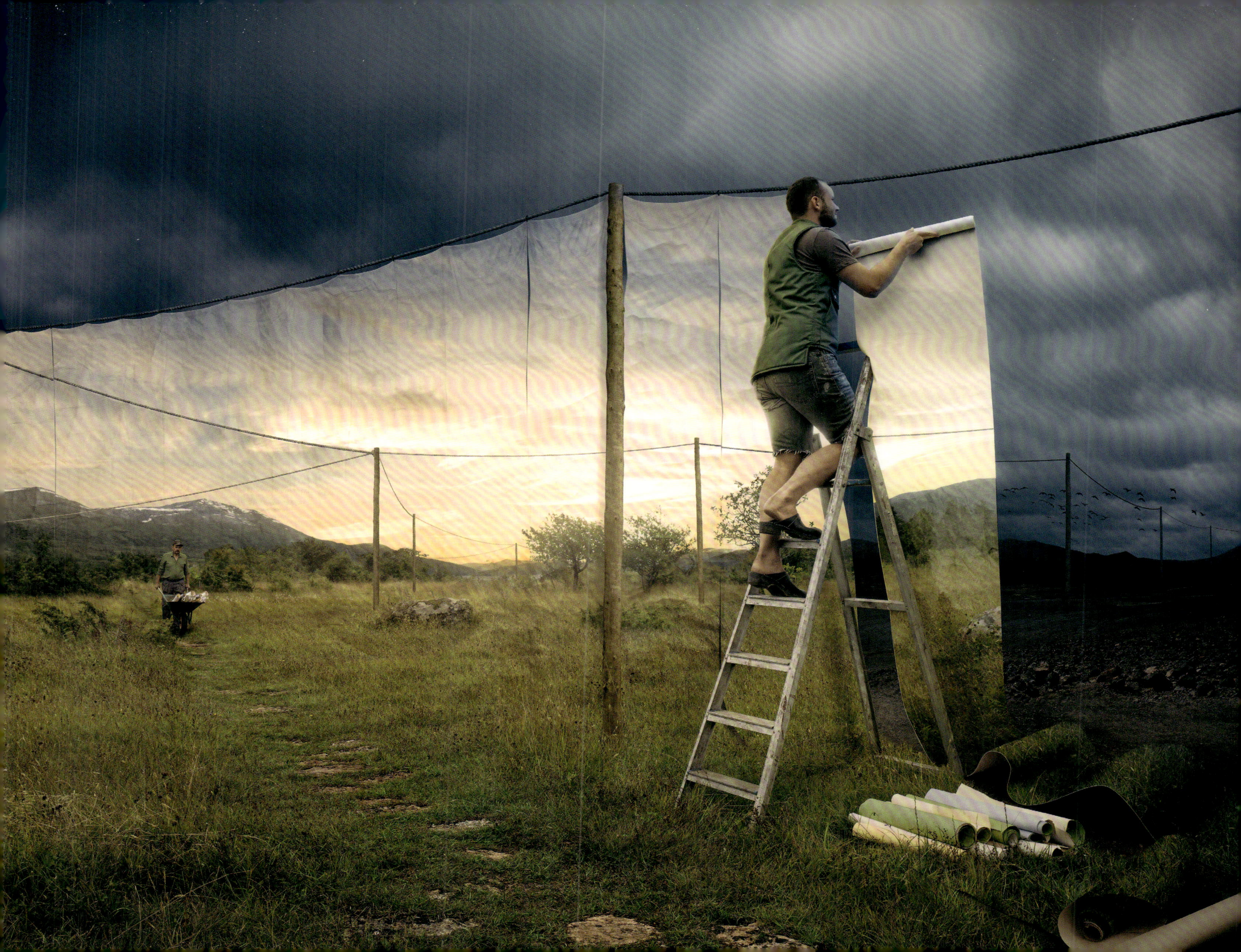

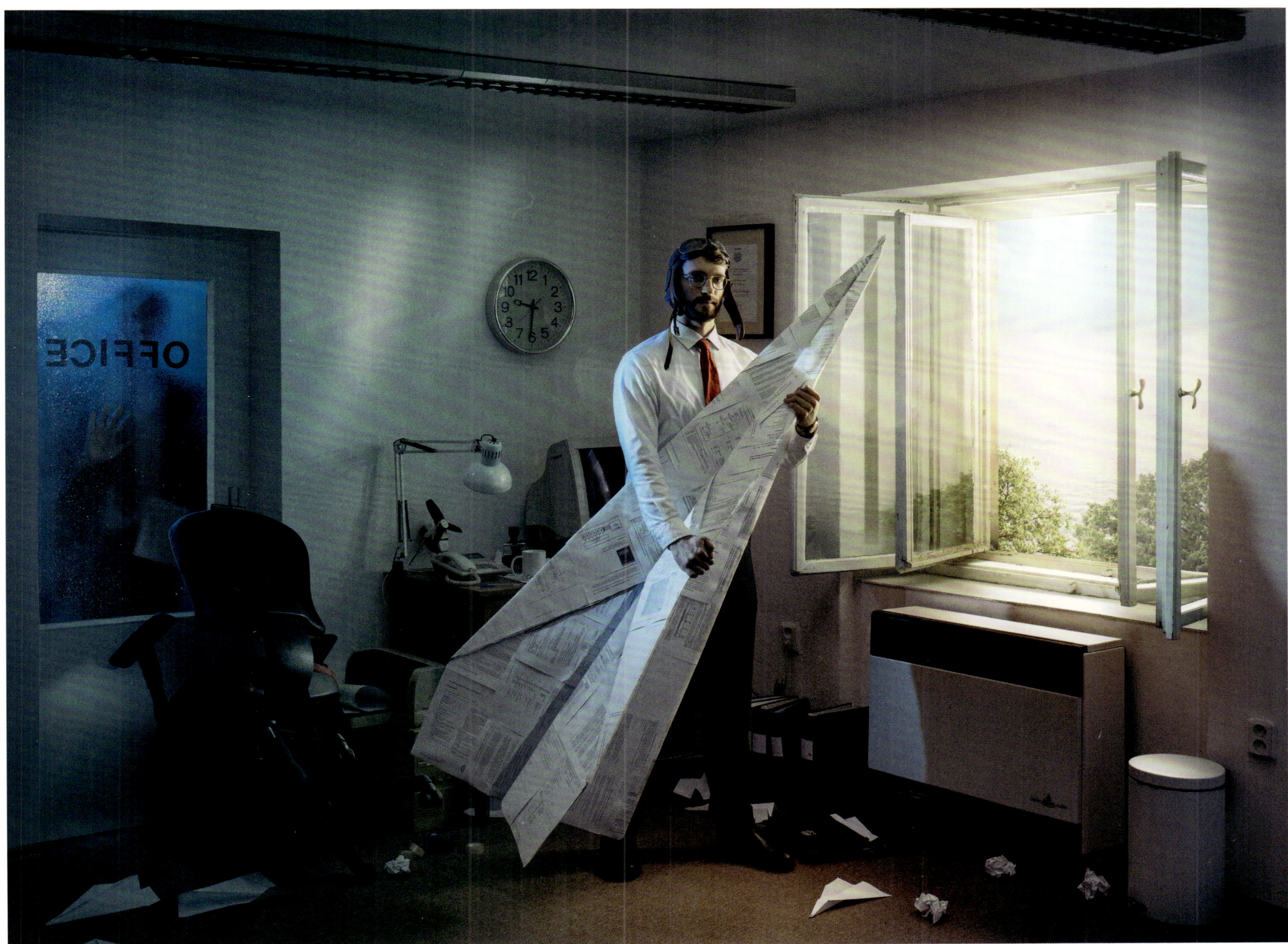

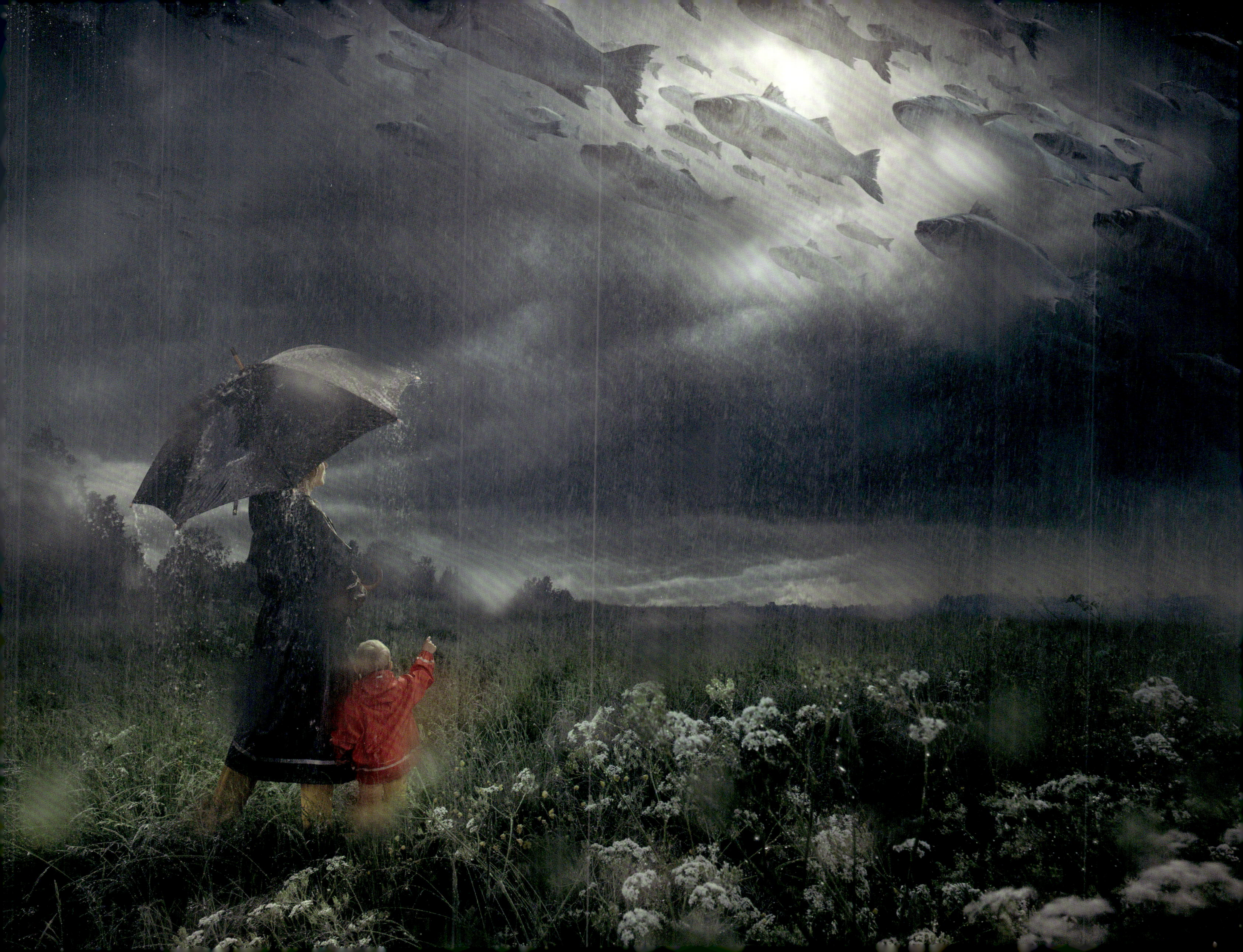

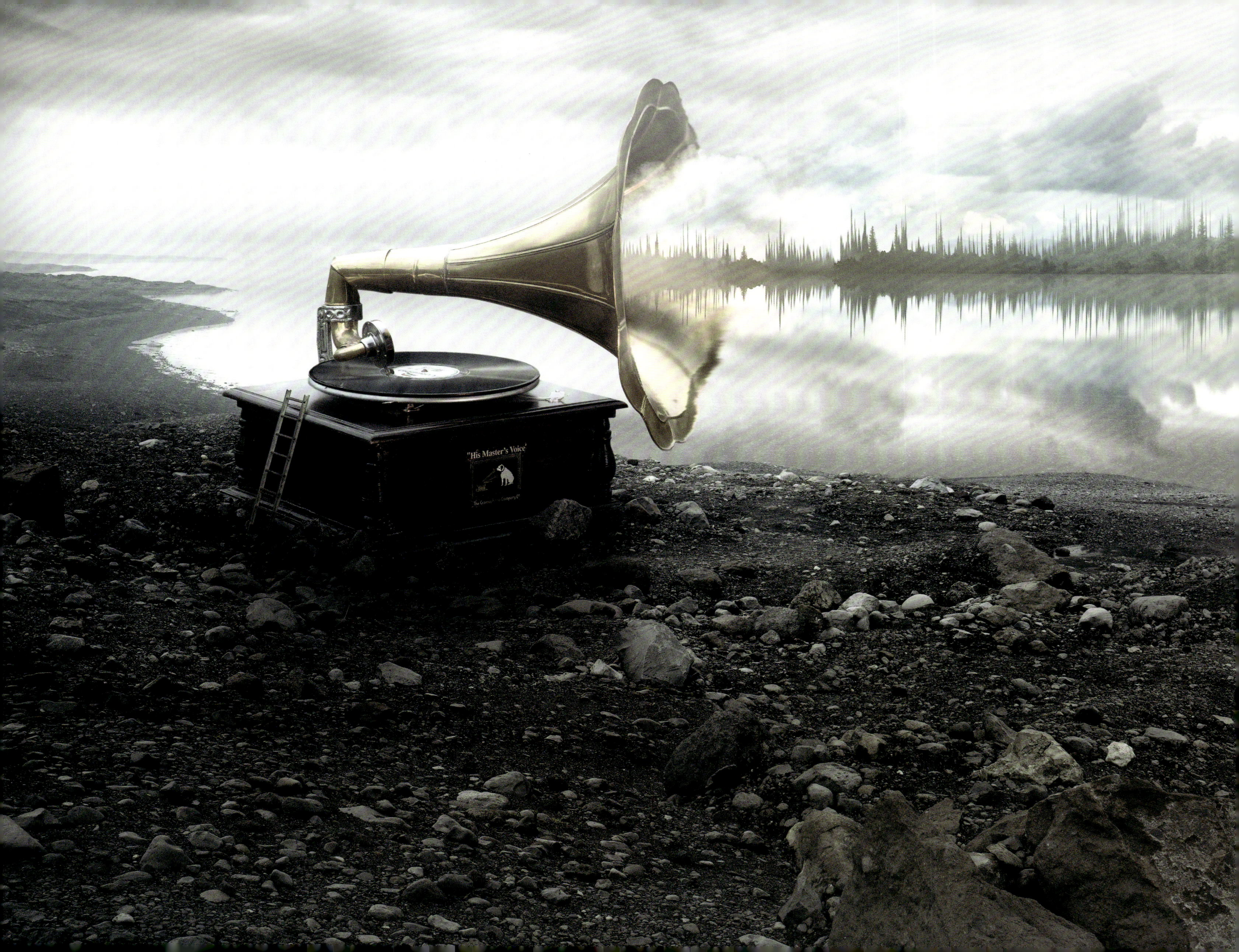

"His Master's Voice"
The Gramophone Company L^{td}

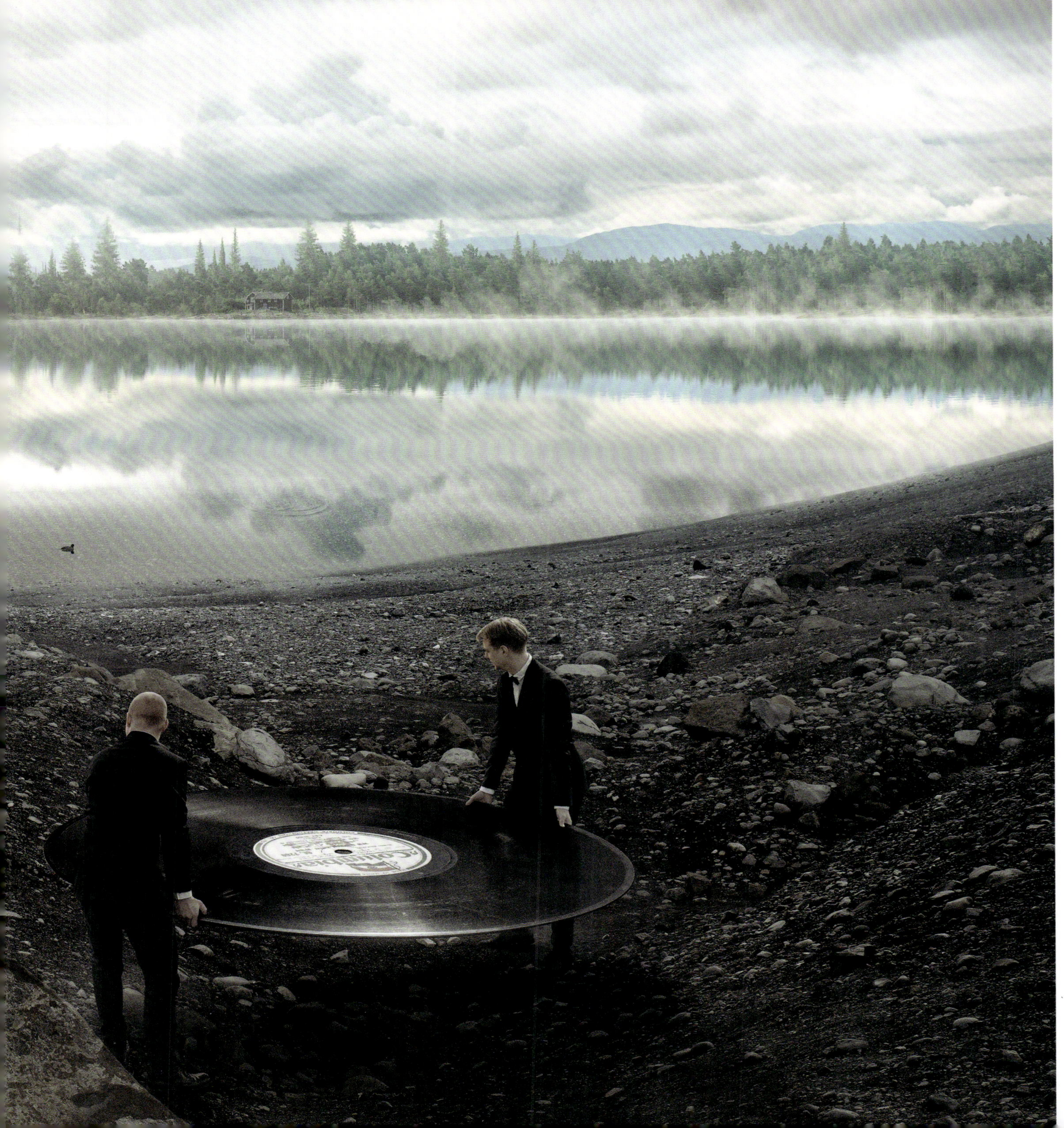

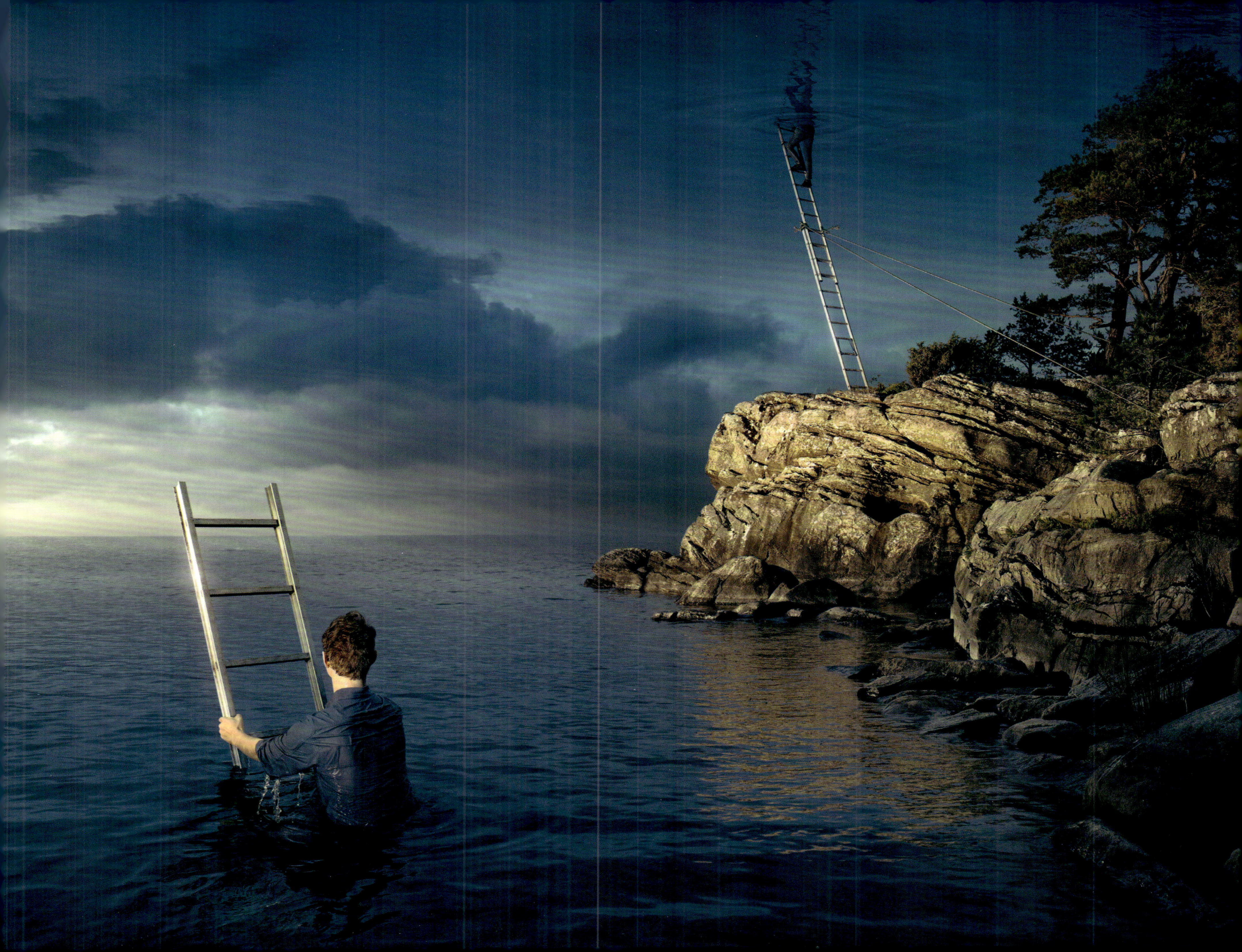

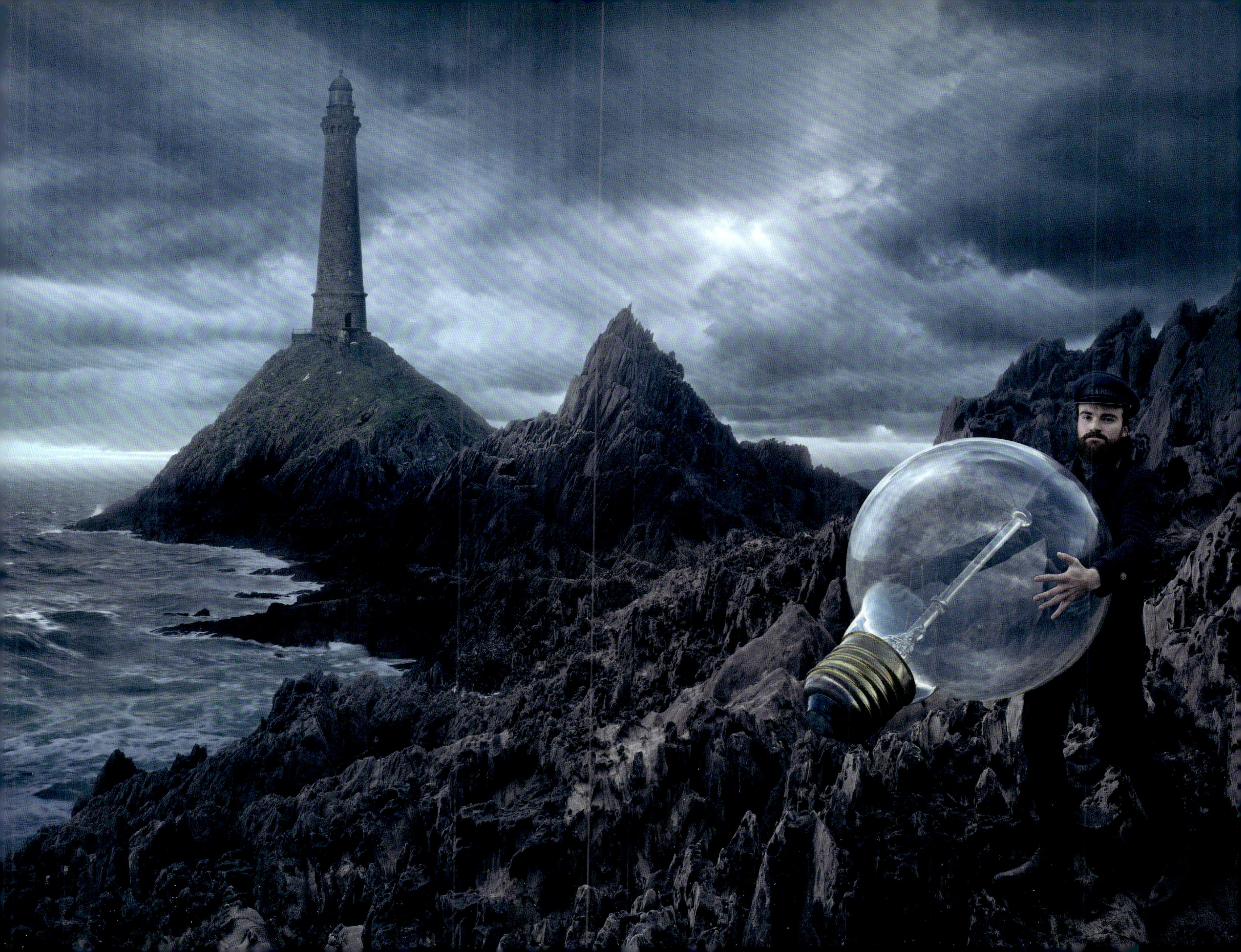

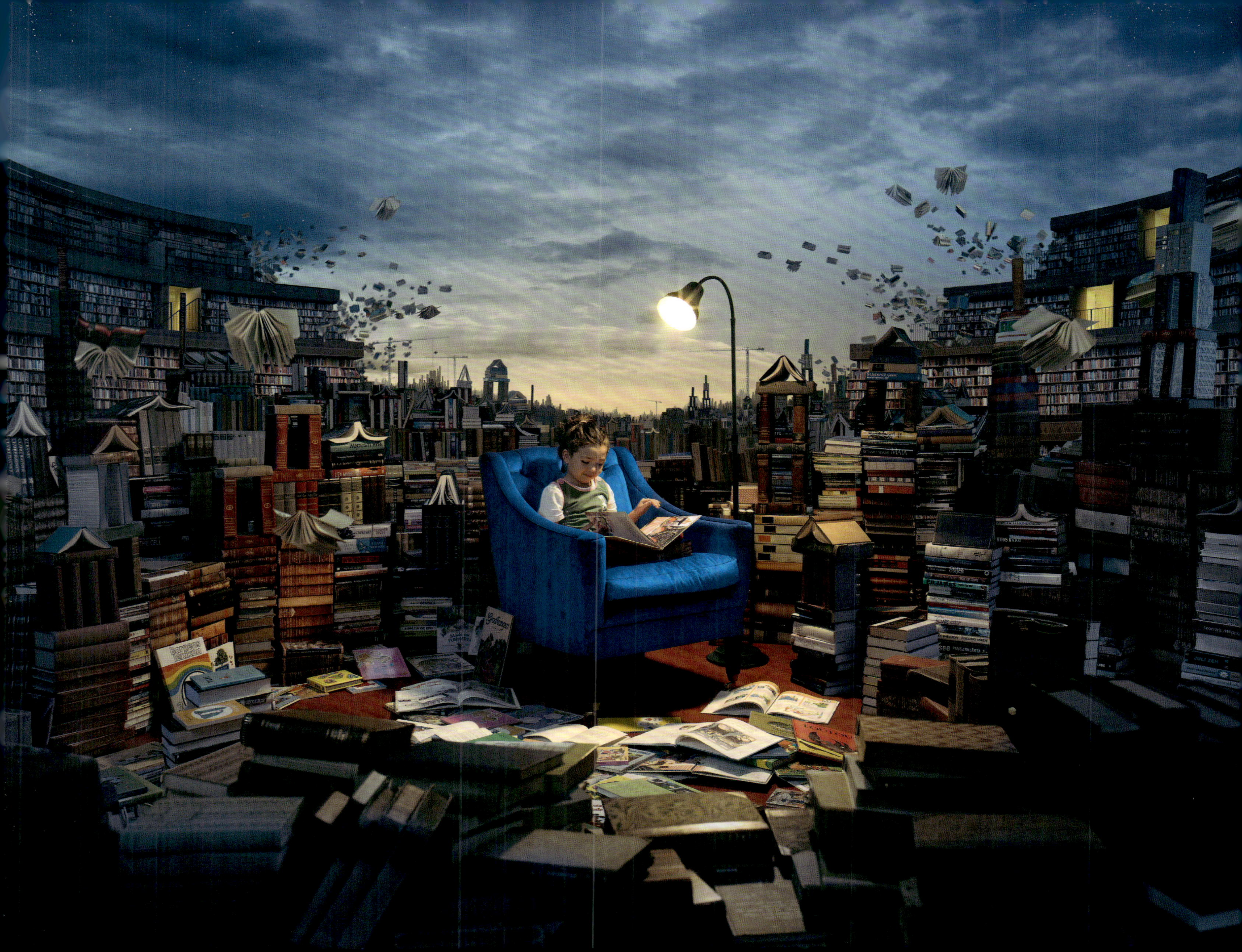

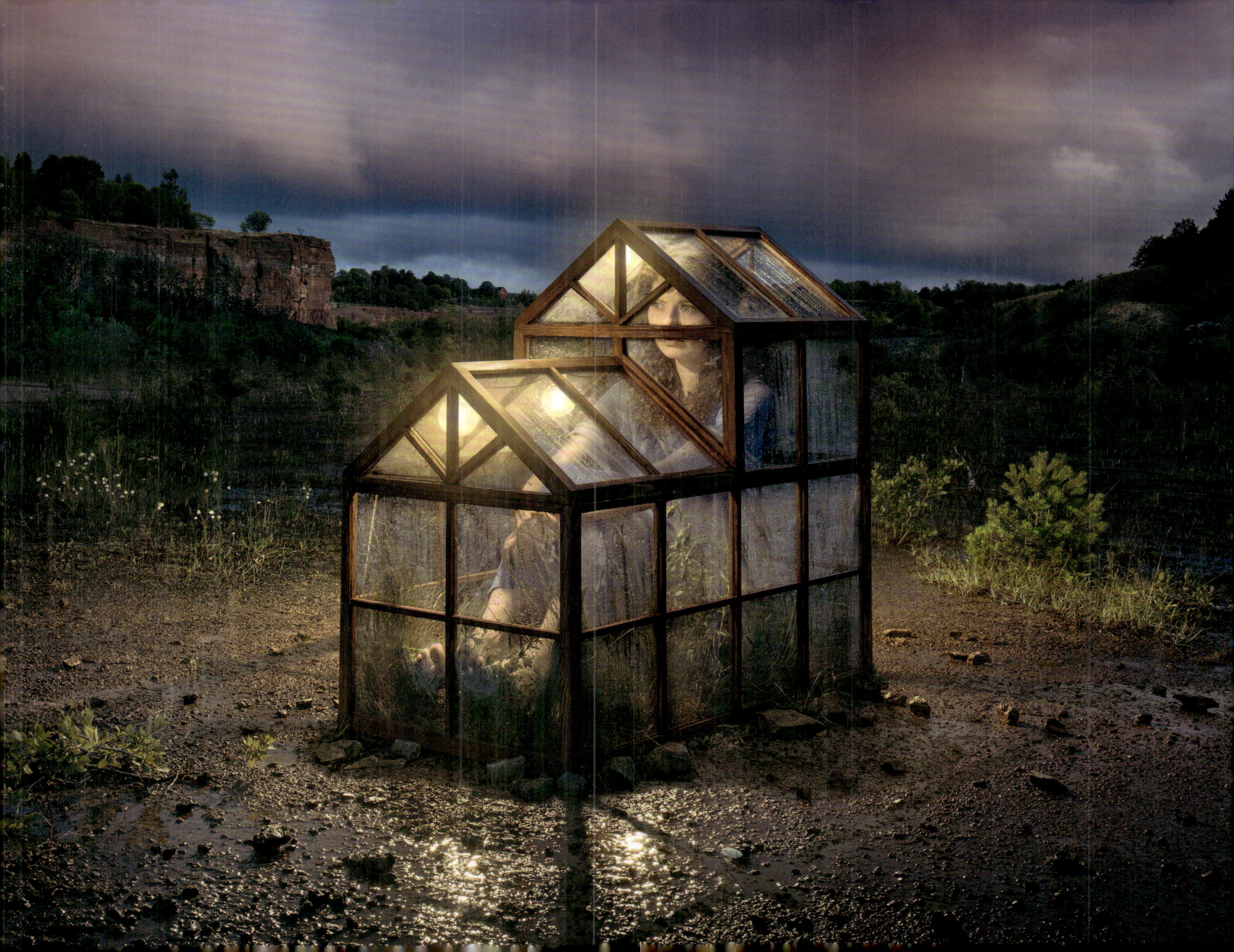

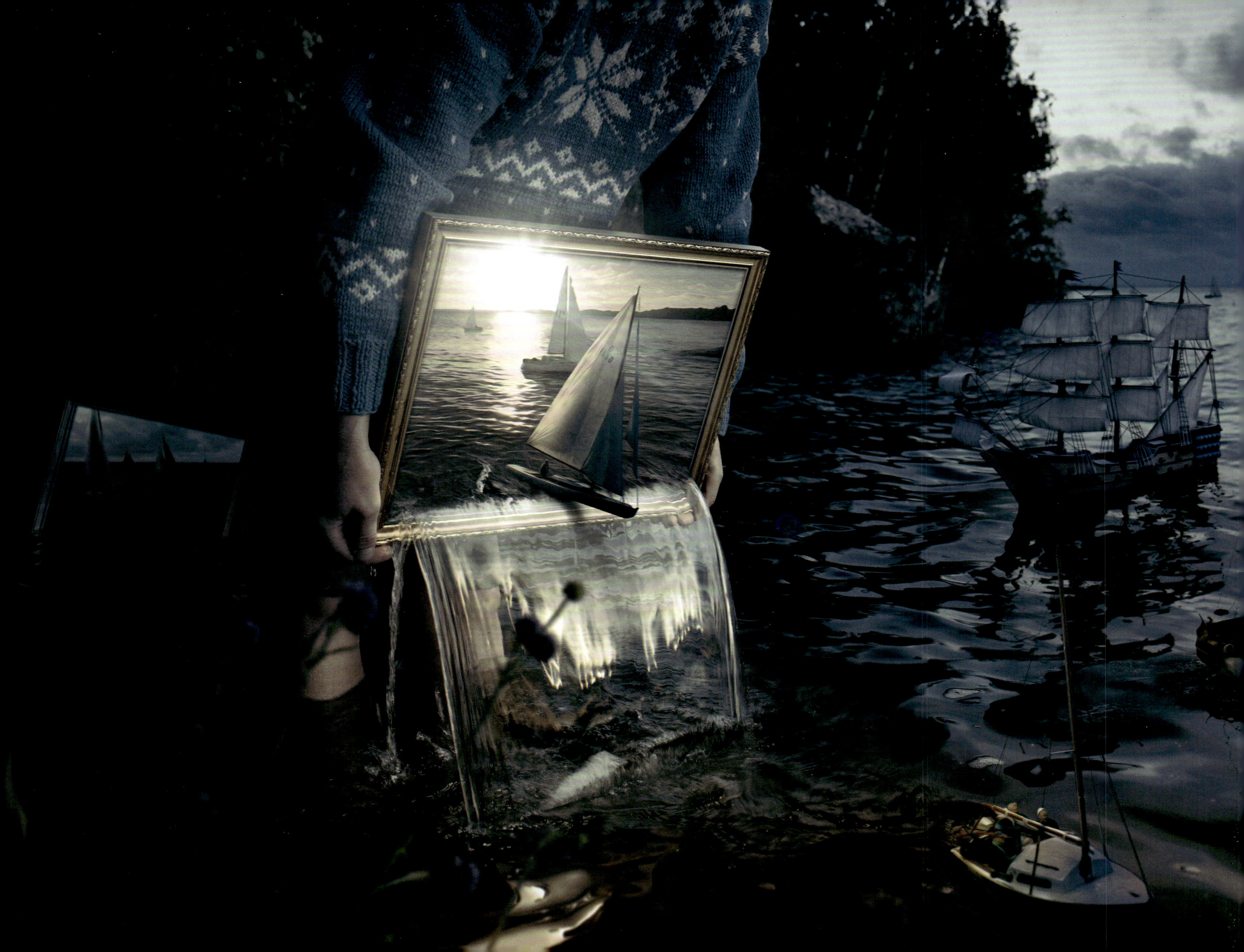

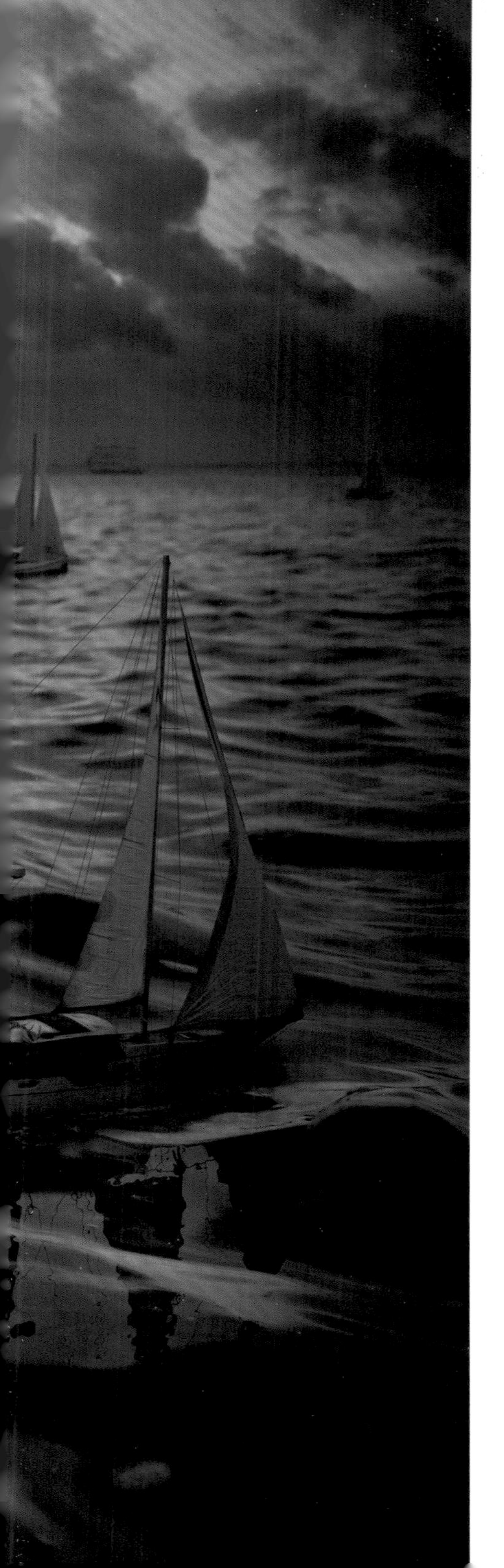

Set Them Free

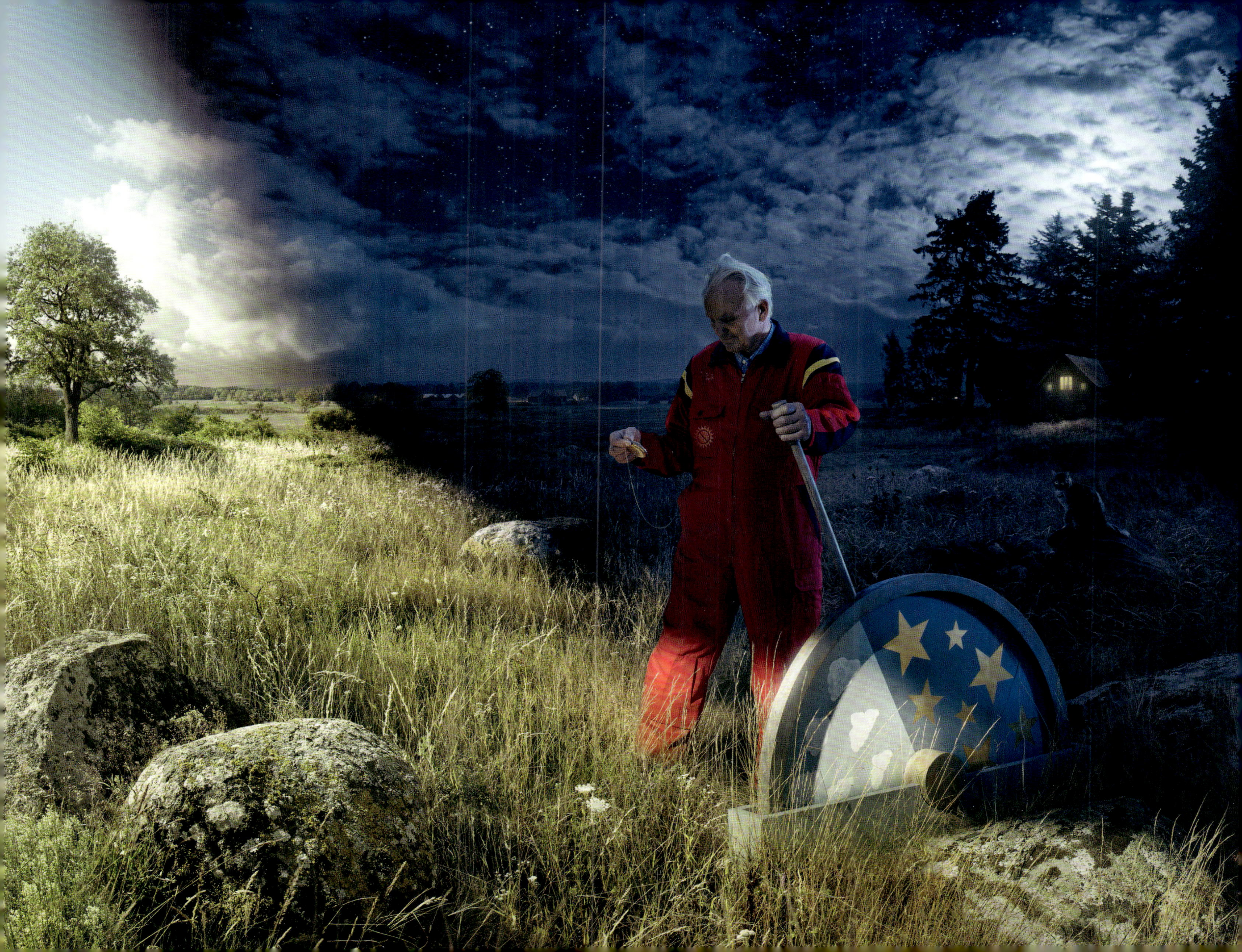

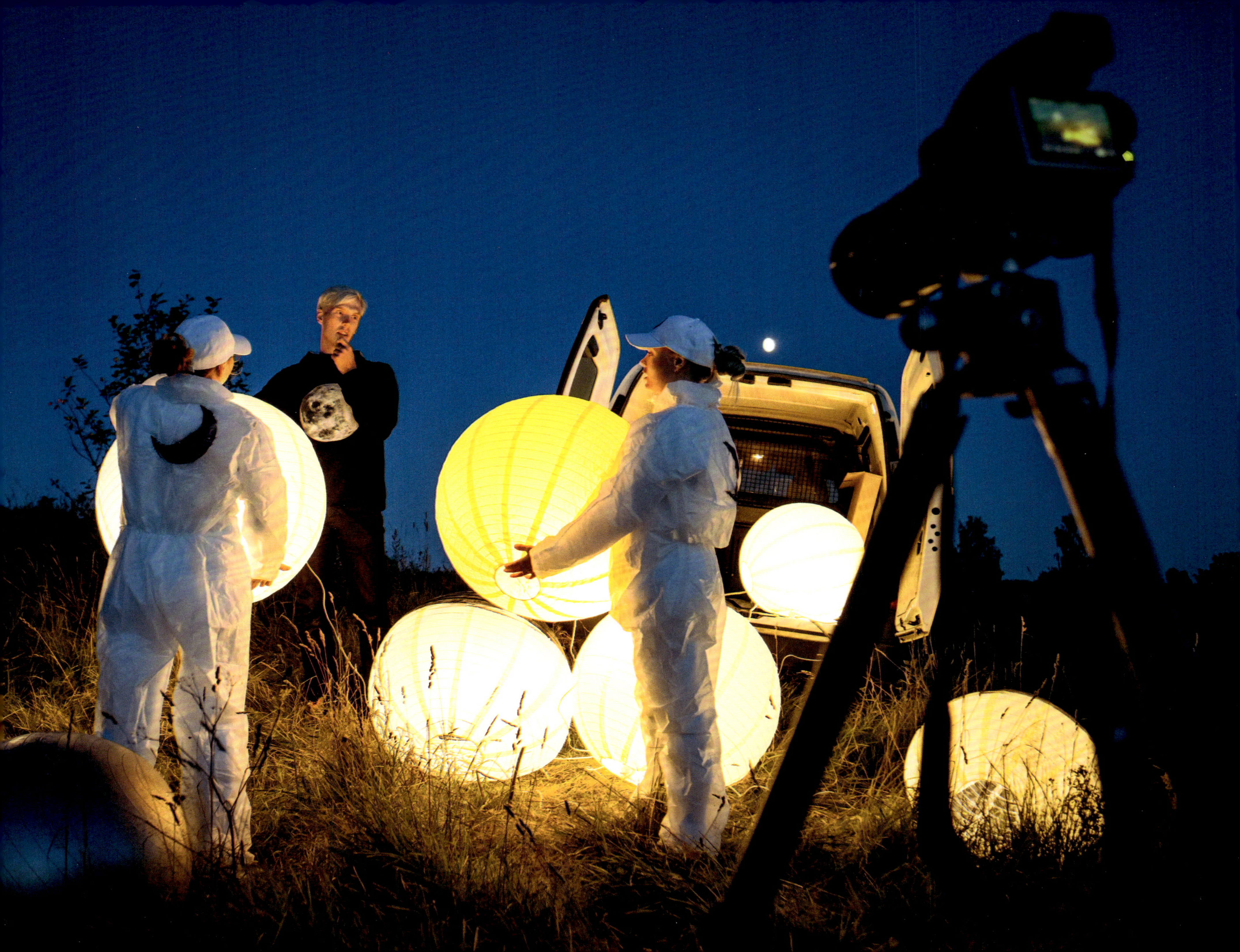

AN AMAZING WORLD OUTSIDE
THE BOUNDS OF TIME AND SPACE

A service company takes care of the full moon at night. Photographer and visual artist
Erik Johansson's world of surrealist images invites viewers to go on a fantastic journey.

Holmestad in south-western Sweden. Broad, sweeping fields of grain and green forests. Traditional, red-painted wooden houses with white trim and white-rendered outbuildings. A rural Swedish idyll. This is where photographer and visual artist Erik Johansson often creates his surrealist images. This is where he grew up. His family's farm is now in the hands of the sixth generation.

"I plan my images at my desk in the studio. Then I photograph them around my family's home. My images are like brief impacts in places around the hamlet of Svenstorp," he said.

Today Erik lives in Prague, but over the years he has also lived in the Swedish cities of Gothenburg and Norrköping, and in Berlin. In recent years his photographs have been exhibited all over the world. Each one takes the viewer on a journey into a fantasy-like world. In "The Forest Library" a girl stands in some tall grass, gazing at an incredible book-filled pavilion. A single ceiling light illuminates an otherwise dark clearing in the woods. Erik creates his images on the computer, starting with anywhere from two to over a hundred photographs. These days he is frequently invited to give talks about his work. Travel and drawing inspiration from new places have always been important to him. Artistic creativity was instilled in him from a young age. His grandmother enjoyed painting in her spare time, and as a child Erik delighted in drawing and creative expression.

"When my mum used to ask me how my day at school had been, I'd draw a comic strip about what had happened to describe the day in pictures. I was around six years old then. I've always liked inventing and creating things," he said.

Erik's parents gave him an inexpensive digital camera for his 15th birthday. "I hadn't asked for one," he said. "But it was a chance to discover digital photography, and a direct way to investigate images and their elements. I could take a photo of a scene and then modify it on the computer."

It was his interest in maths, however, that steered him towards studying at Chalmers University of Technology in Gothenburg. Several of his school friends were heading to Gothenburg for their studies, and he immersed himself in student life. Photography was put on the back burner in favour of computer programming, until a few years later when a friend bought a digital DSLR camera. Erik immediately saw the difference in image quality compared to his own camera and that it offered opportunities. His interest in photography was reawakened.

"I liked the creativity behind coding," he said, "but it wasn't as visual as working with photography or drawing. So after I got a chance to try out my friend's camera, I bought myself the same model."

That was in 2007. All of his work was still done as a hobby. "One of my goals was to see how good I could get at twisting reality yet still feel like it was a photograph. I built up the images in Photoshop. Tried things out. Felt my way forward," he said.

He learned from his mistakes. Learned how the camera worked. What he could adjust afterwards on the computer. Which elements – like depth of field and lighting – had to be in place at the photo shoot so that he could combine the images. It took several years to acquire the skills to really achieve what he wanted. His first commercial job was for a company that sold swimming pools.

"Gradually I started to think this was a career to focus on," he said.

He achieved the best results when he took the photos that would make up the final image himself and had control over the entire production chain. Meanwhile, his own projects were taking up more of his time. When he uploaded 20 or so images to an international photography forum, it resulted in a mini-explosion of interest in his work. In 2011 Erik got a phone call asking if he wanted to give a talk at the fifth TED Salon in London where the theme was "Travels in Space, Time & Imagination".

"Of course I said yes," he recalled. "At that time I was living in Norrköping and had started getting a few more international commissions. This was definitely a key milestone in my career."

Erik has been able to continue investing in more advanced cameras and computers. Today he works with a Hasselblad H6D-50c. He has also had the luxury of allowing each image to emerge over time. In many cases, the idea has been around for quite a while: first as a quick sketch – simple lines and figures – in a drawing app on his phone, then as a more detailed drawing he hangs on the wall above the desk in his studio. It might stay there for a couple of years.

"I usually note the year on each sketch," he explained. "I did the sketch for one image I'm working on now two years ago. For me, time is the only way to understand which of my sketches are of interest. Choosing the narrative and capturing the right moment in that story are a large part of the work. The title is a clue."

It can take him up to a year or longer to create an image from start to finish. Finding props. Models. The right location and angle to make the final image true to life. Then he assembles everything in Photoshop. Generates a seamless whole from all the components. Erik likes constraints. They necessitate coming up with creative solutions with the resources that are available.

"I'm always photographing different skies and trees to save in my digital archive," he said. "I never purchase photos from stock photo libraries or create them using CGI. My raw material is photos I've taken myself."

He added: "The camera is the best tool we have for depicting reality. My images look like ordinary photographs, but they contain surrealistic, unreal elements. I always try to include a human element in my images, so they resemble our reality."

Our interview took place when Erik was on a brief visit to Stockholm, having recently returned to Sweden from an exhibition at Seoul Arts Center in South Korea. He had spent much of the past six months travelling. He said he had clocked up 110 days away. Next up was a conference in São Paulo, Brazil. His second show at Stockholm's Fotografiska museum will open in December. His commercial agent takes bookings for two or three commissions a year. Other than that, he works on his own projects. He has learned to travel light, at least when he returns to Sweden for work.

"I've got two wardrobes of clothes, one in Prague and one at my parents' place in Svenstorp," he said. "So basically I just bring my camera and toothbrush."

Our coffee cups were empty. Somewhere a clock struck three. It was a very warm day in late summer.

"You shouldn't be afraid to make mistakes," Erik summed up. "I'd encourage everybody to go out and to create more. It would make the world a better place."

Anna Henriksson

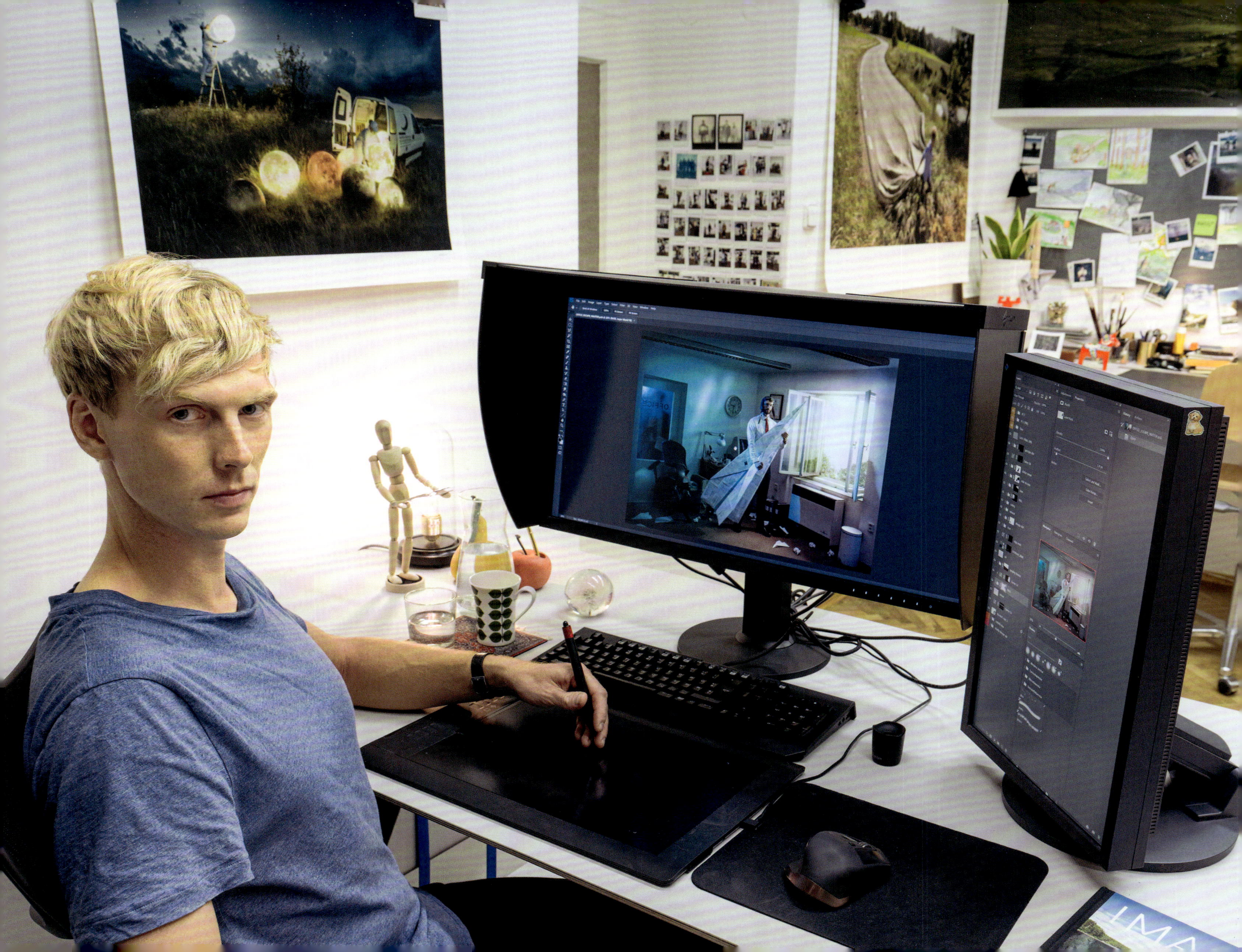

BEHIND THE SCENES

There are no limits to our imagination. My images are an attempt to capture the impossible.

To retain some realism and get as close to reality as possible without computer-generated or illustrated elements, I have to find ways to capture all the parts of the images with my camera. Sometimes I end up building specially designed props; other times I come up with simple tools and surfaces that are reminiscent of others, which enable me to create a seamless transition between the various elements of an image. It's a painstaking process that requires finding the perfect location and a suitable model, then combining all the pieces of the puzzle to complete the image. Although each image exists in its own universe, Swedish and northern European settings are a consistent motif in my images.

I always have several projects on the go simultaneously, because otherwise I wouldn't be very productive. On average, I manage to produce around eight images per year. I am constantly improving my skills with the tools I use, which makes me more efficient, but at the same time I am always seeking out new challenges and looking to produce more complex ideas.

In most cases I physically construct as much as possible of the setting I want to capture. That makes it easier for the models to relate to and interact with the universe I want to create for each image. Ultimately it's also more faithful to reality. Light and perspective are the key factors in creating the illusion of a unitary whole.

What happens before the sun comes up? What if the sun was not a huge ball of fire the Earth orbits around? Imagine it was just hovering below the edge of the horizon, waiting to rise.

This idea emerged from those musings. Straight away I thought about a place near the old stone quarry at Kinnekulle, near Lake Vänern in south-western Sweden. There's a meadow that ends at the edge of a sheer 10-metre-high cliff, which would be the perfect setting. To capture a sense of belonging and scale, the image also needed a person – maybe someone out walking their dog. Someone who just happened to take a detour from their usual route and ended up at that cliff edge just as the sun was starting to come up.

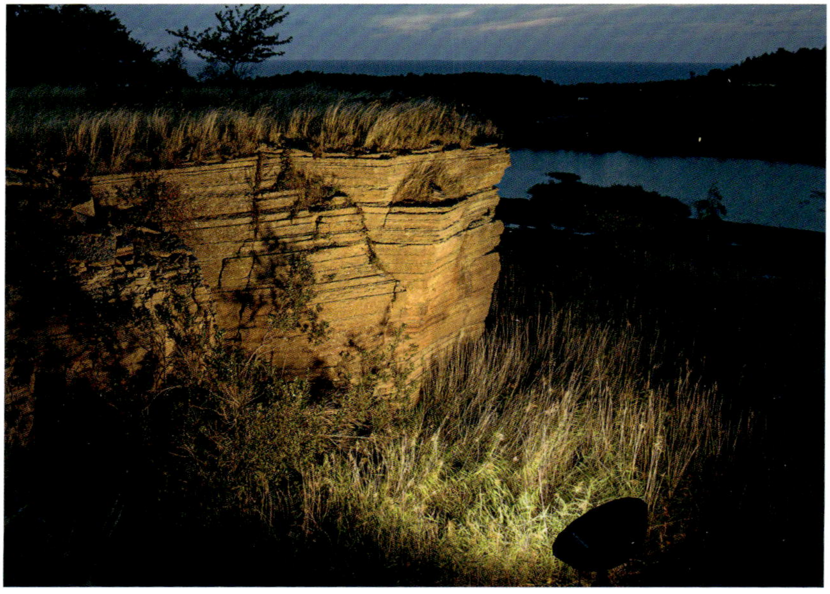

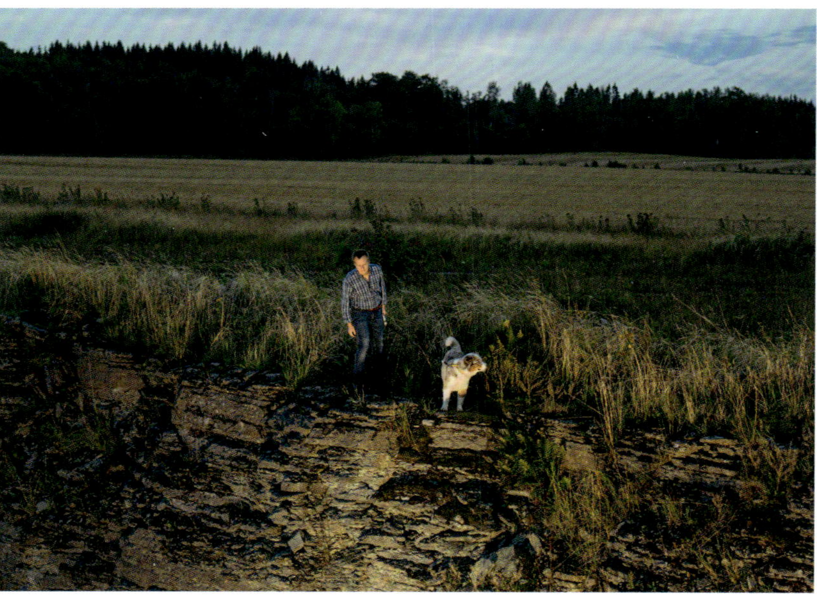

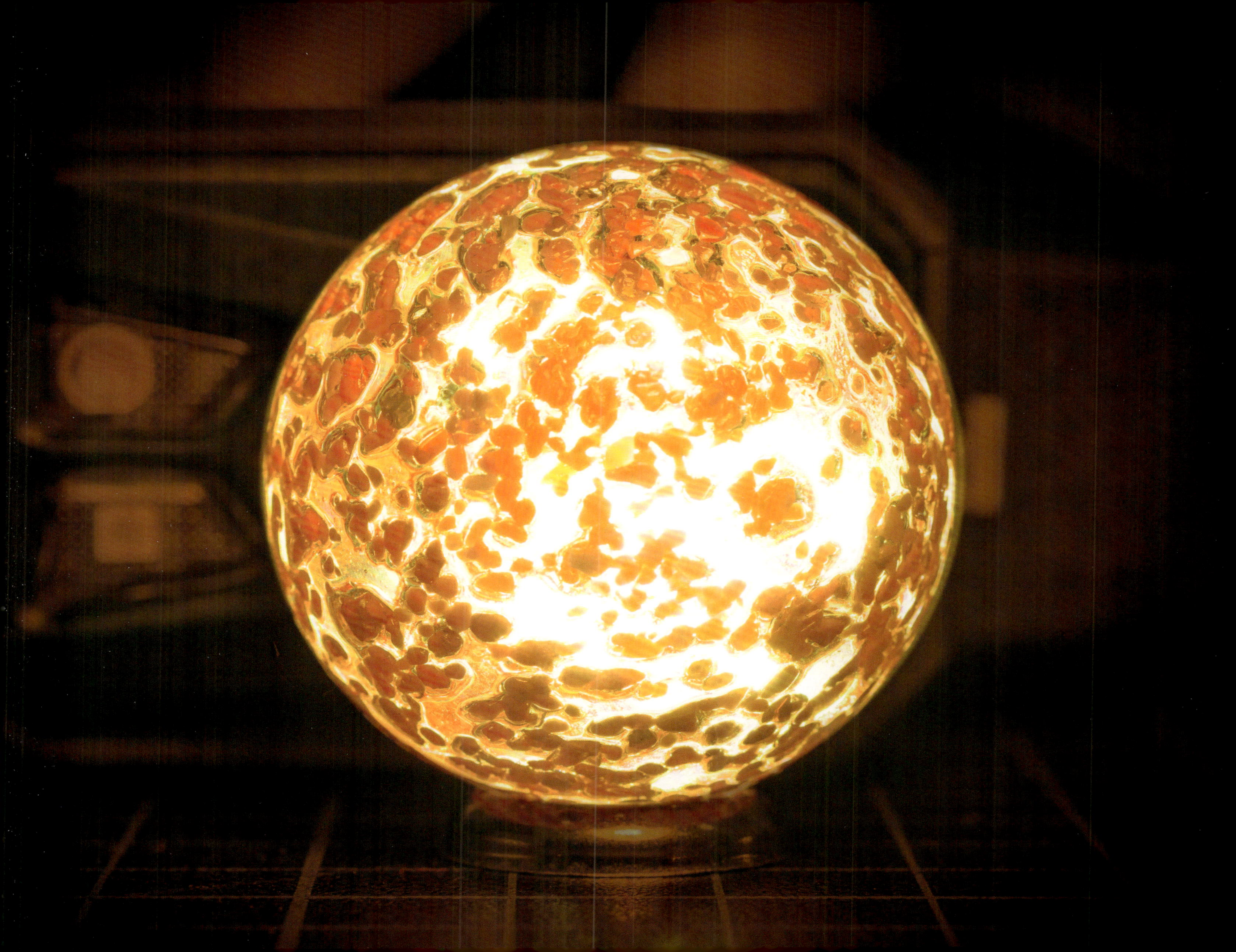

This idea arose largely from the news stories of recent years – the notion that something is wrong with the world. We need a reset, an emergency stop or something to bring the world back on track again. I thought everyone could relate to a big red button with a protective glass dome. Its bright red colour indicates it's a very important button, for whatever reason. Two people are working together to dig up the button, as if it has been hidden for many years, but now it's time for action.

I could have found a smaller button to photograph and then scaled it up afterwards to make it appear supersized. But instead I decided to build a full-scale button that could be pressed. I thought it would be easier for the models to relate to the story if they had a real button to interact with. When something actually exists, that also makes it easier to create realism. Of course it's more difficult and time-consuming to dig a big hole and put a giant button in it, but the end result is better and it actually saves a lot of time in post-production.

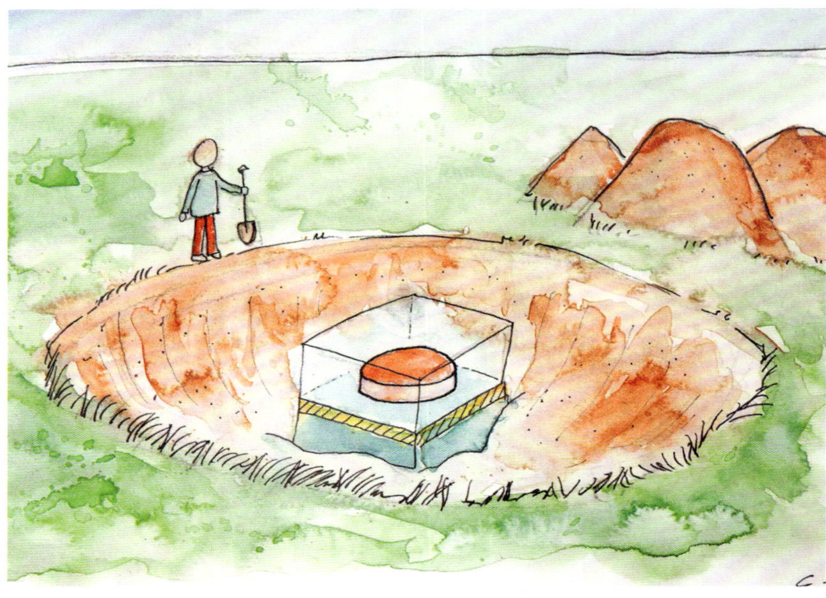

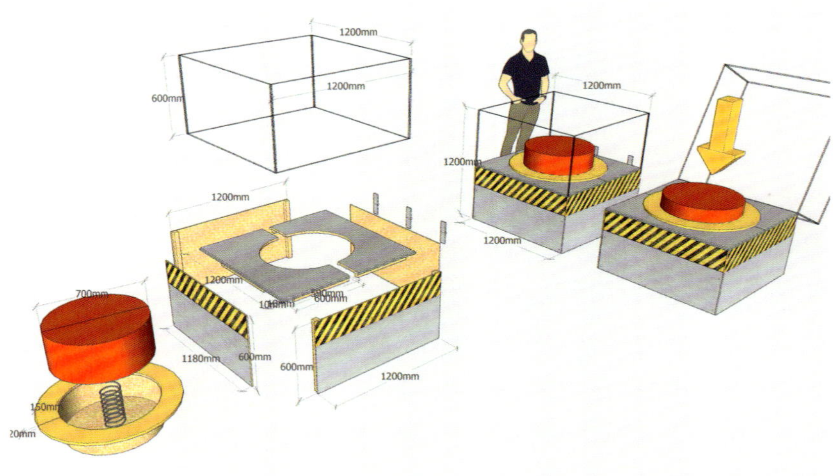

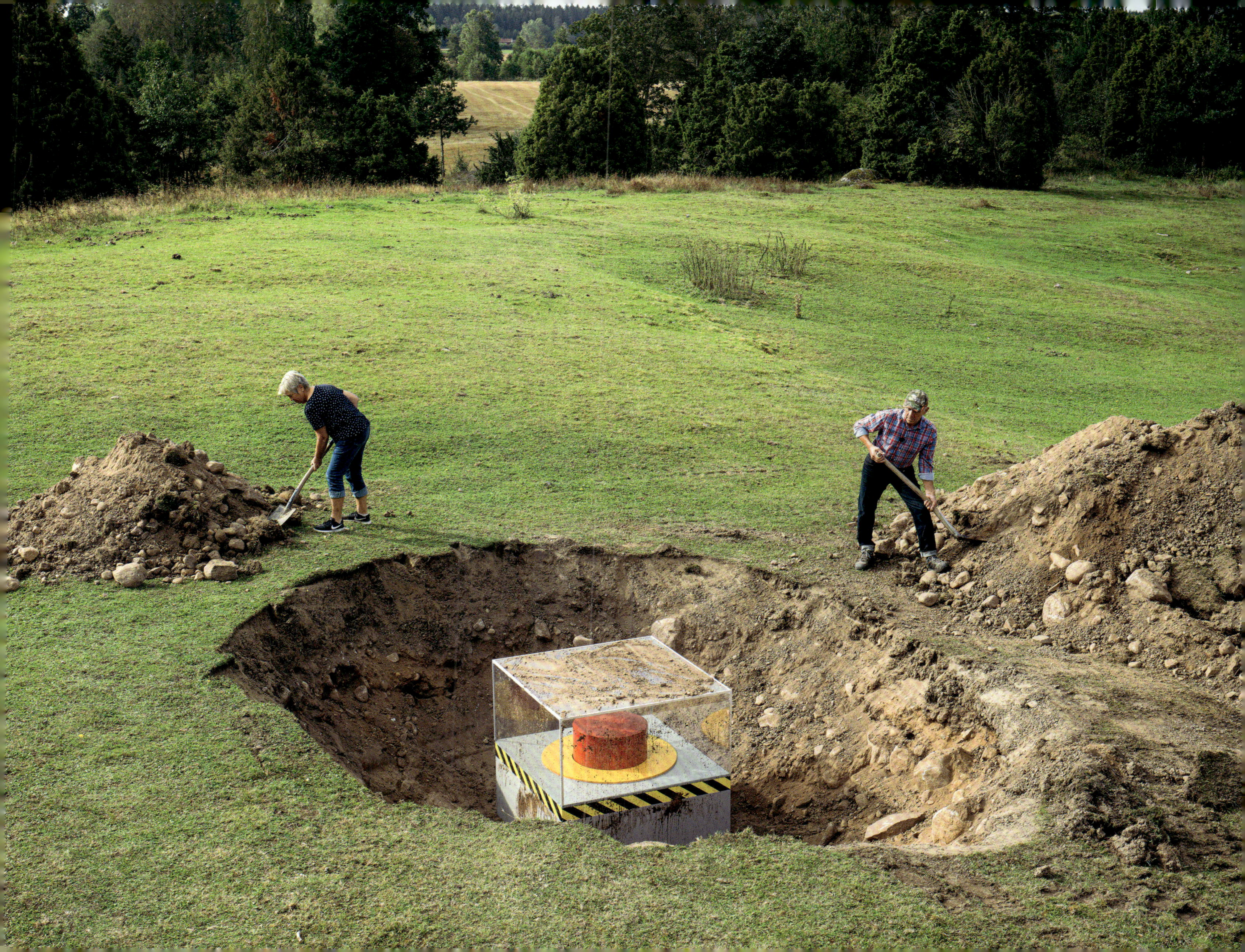

W̲hat is the man with the axe planning to do? He seems determined to chop down the burning tree, even though the obvious solution would be to douse the fire with water. Does he know something we don't?

In order to get the message across, it was important to make the tree look like it was really on fire. I didn't want to burn a healthy tree, but after some research I found a dead tree that was going to be cut down. I got permission to set it on fire. With help from the local fire brigade and a special-effects team, I wrapped the tree in fabric soaked in flammable liquid to generate plenty of flames. I had found the hill a few months previously and photographed it with flashes using warm filters, to show that the burning tree was illuminating the areas around the hilltop.

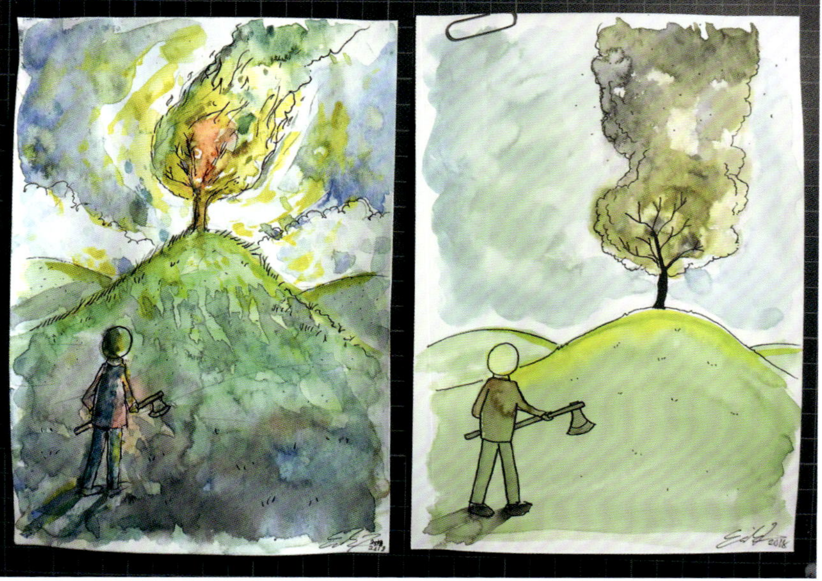

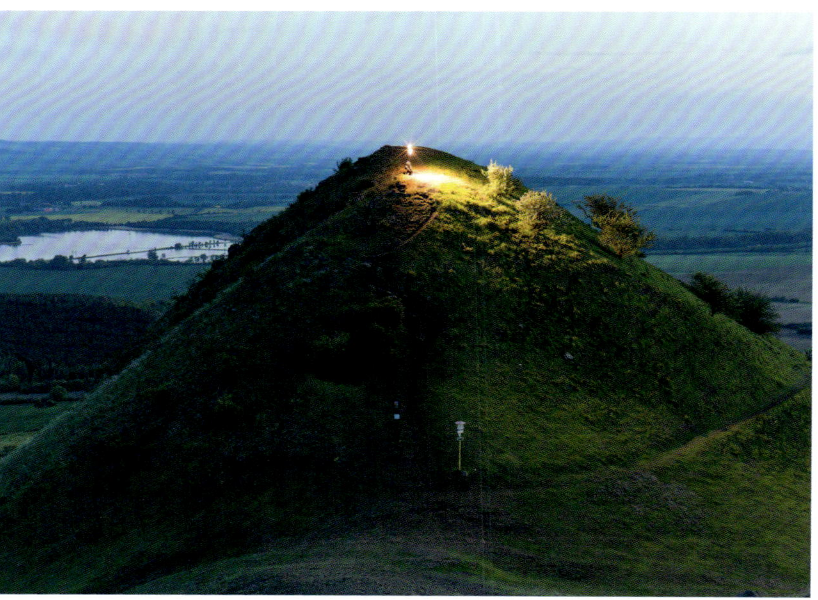

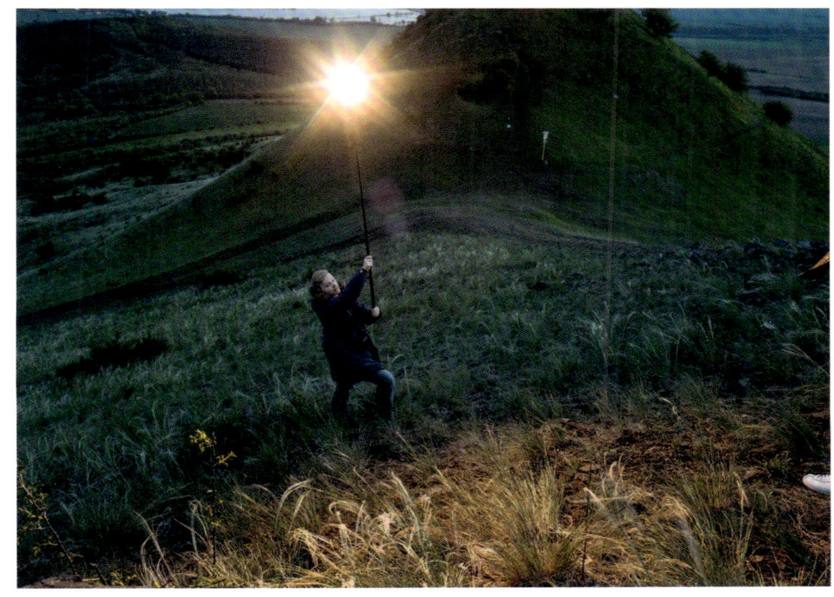

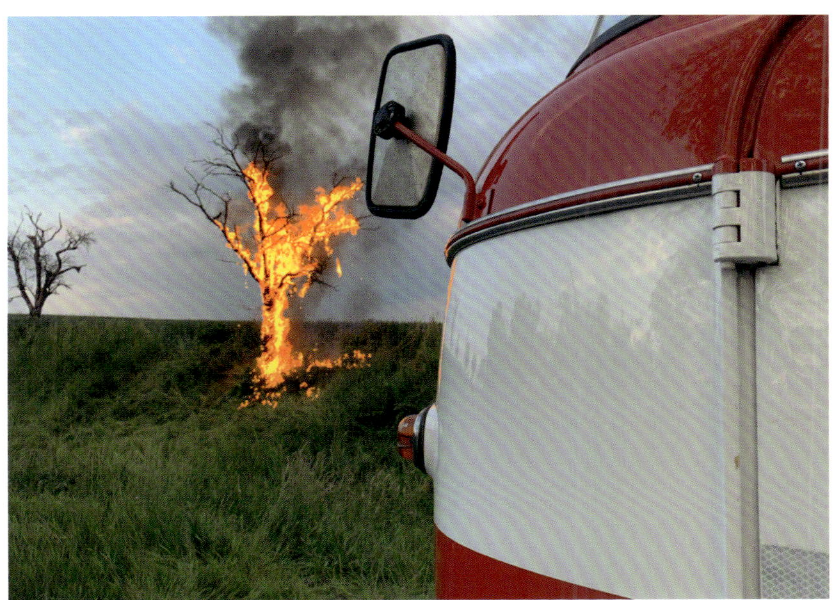

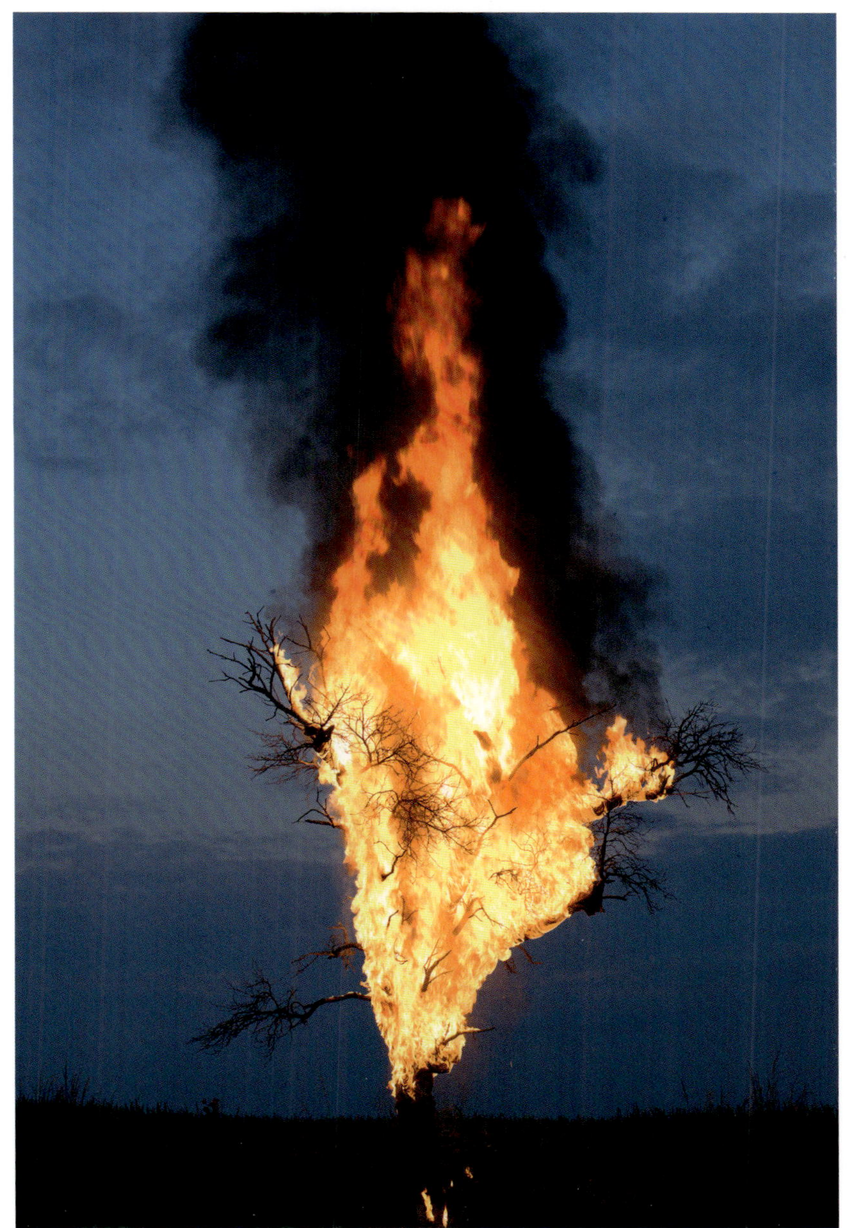

We probably all have our own comfort zone where we feel safe and secure. A zone we don't like to leave unless we have to. I wanted to investigate the idea of our comfort zone in an image. I thought even if we've chosen a place to stay in ourselves, it can also constitute a sort of prison. I wanted to create something that looks like a safe, comfortable place that's also claustrophobic and prison-like, with something beyond the horizon that might have something to offer, if only we ventured to step outside.

I imagined a house-like structure with a person trapped and locked up. A greenhouse would be ideal for showing the person inside. I took the measurements of a seated person and built a simple wooden structure to get an idea of how it looked. When I was happy with the dimensions of the structure, I contacted a couple of carpenters who specialise in building props for films and theatre productions. I gave them a detailed diagram with dimensions, and a few weeks later I had my custom-built greenhouse. I photographed the greenhouse and model in a quarry.

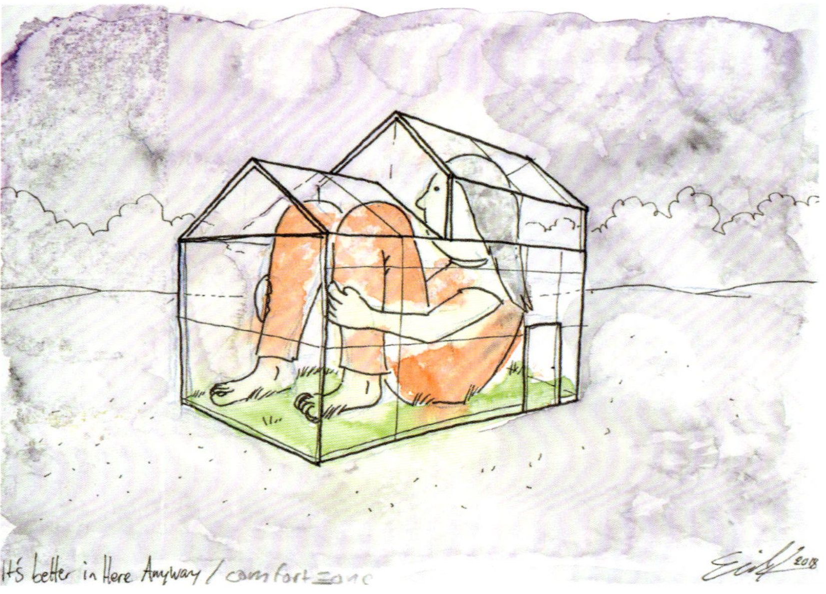

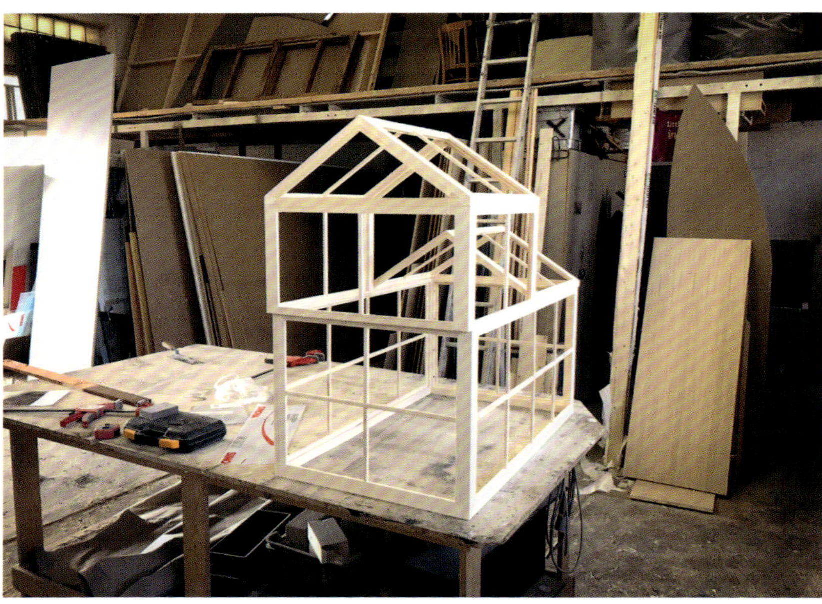

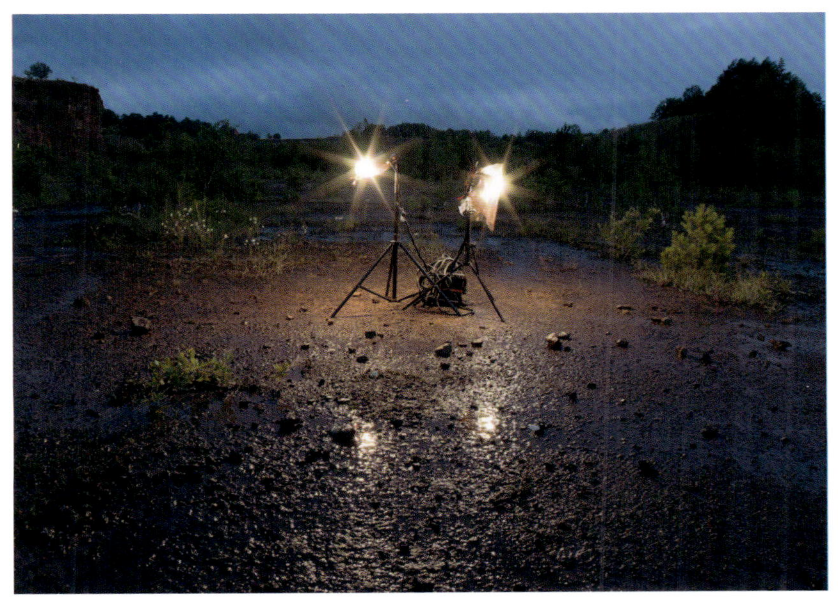

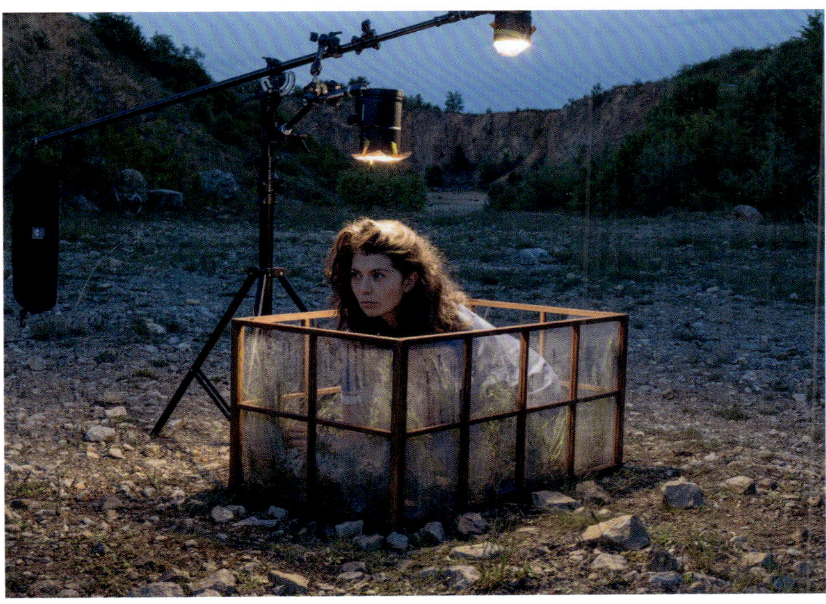

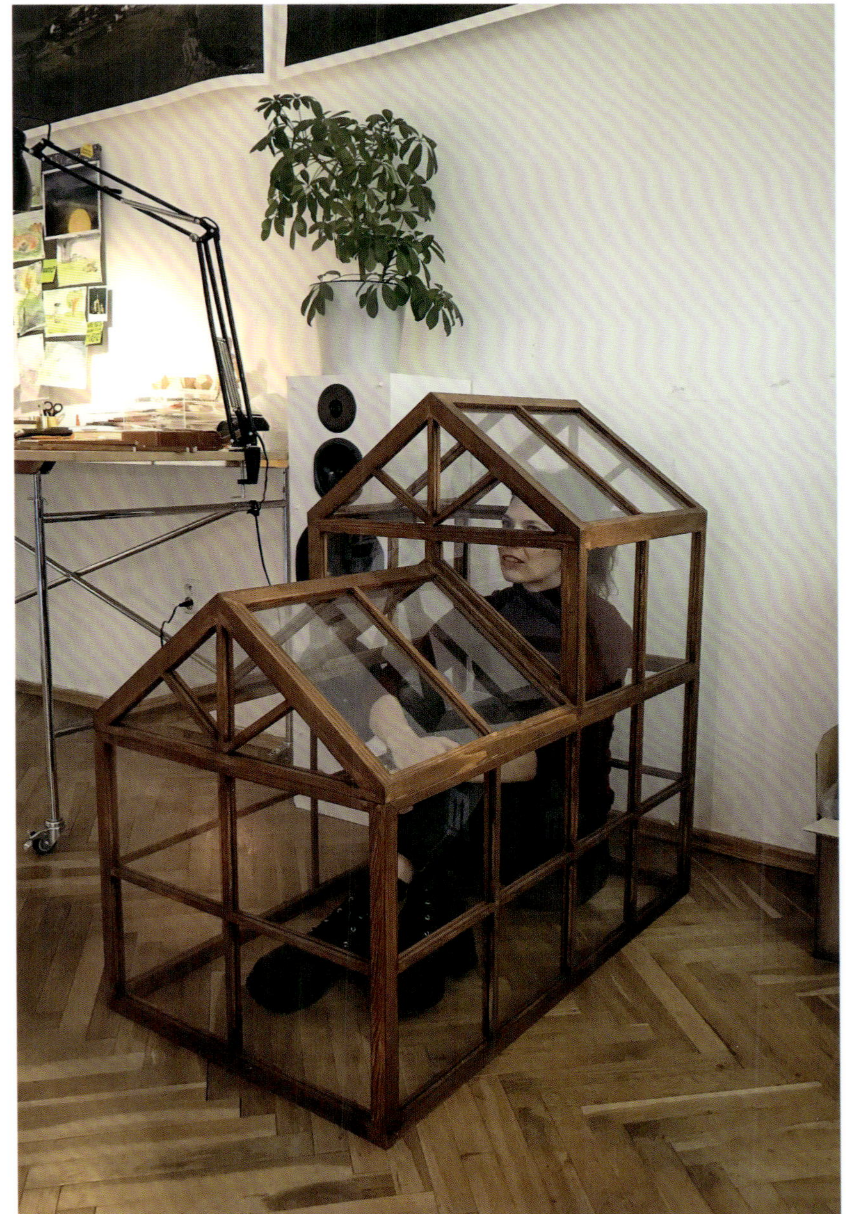

Does the moon have to be a big rock that orbits the Earth? What if the moon was something that was replaced every evening by a moon service team? They'd probably need a van to transport the different moons, along with tools and protective gear to avoid contaminating them. All these little details take a long time to consider, but they often contribute to the narrative I want to communicate in my images.

One evening in late summer I drove a van out into the countryside with two models and a bunch of rice-paper lanterns. As the evening light faded, the light from the lanterns grew stronger. I waited to find a perfect balance in the light and the positions of the models. The image was largely created in the camera. Later I replaced the lanterns with moon surfaces and added a few more stars and clouds to the clear, empty sky we had at the shoot.

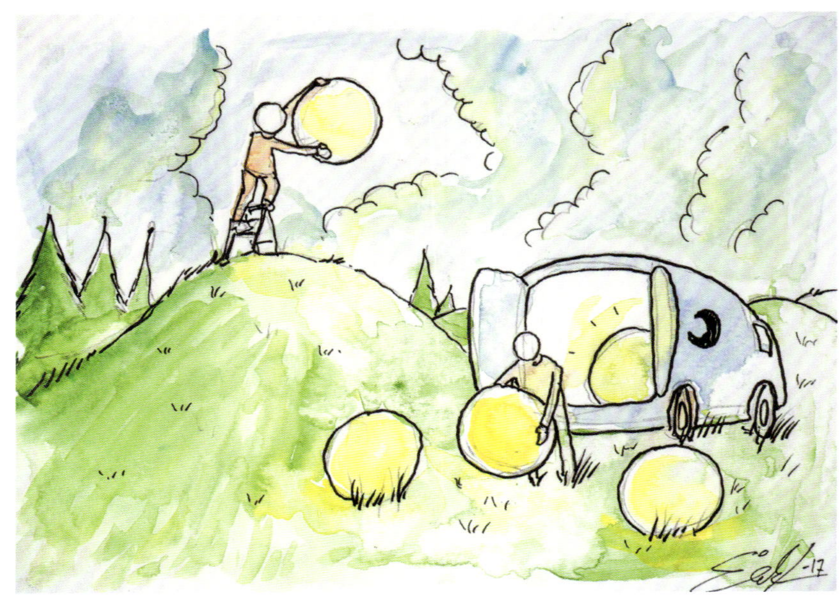

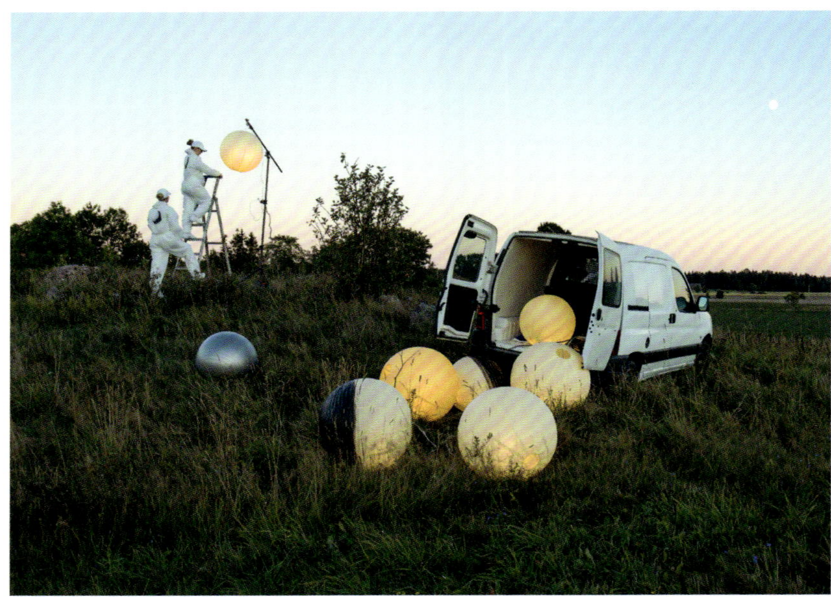

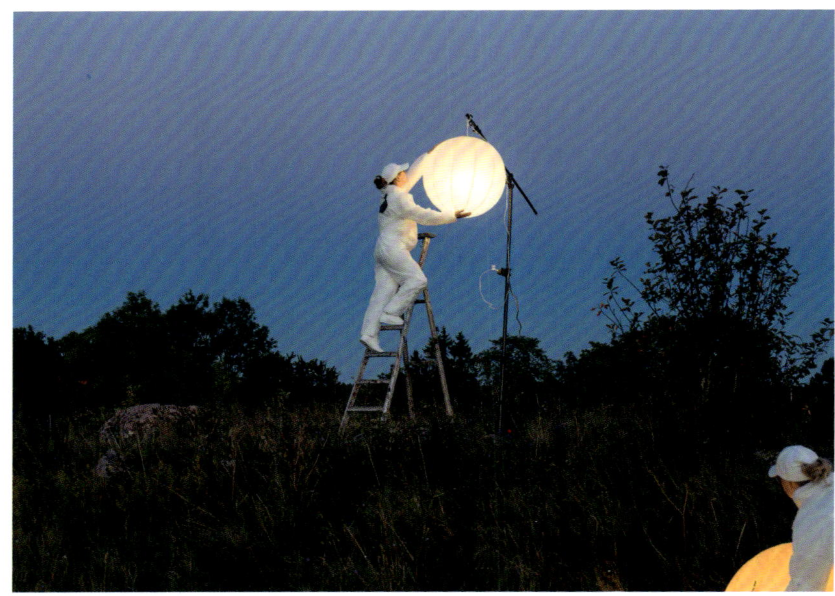

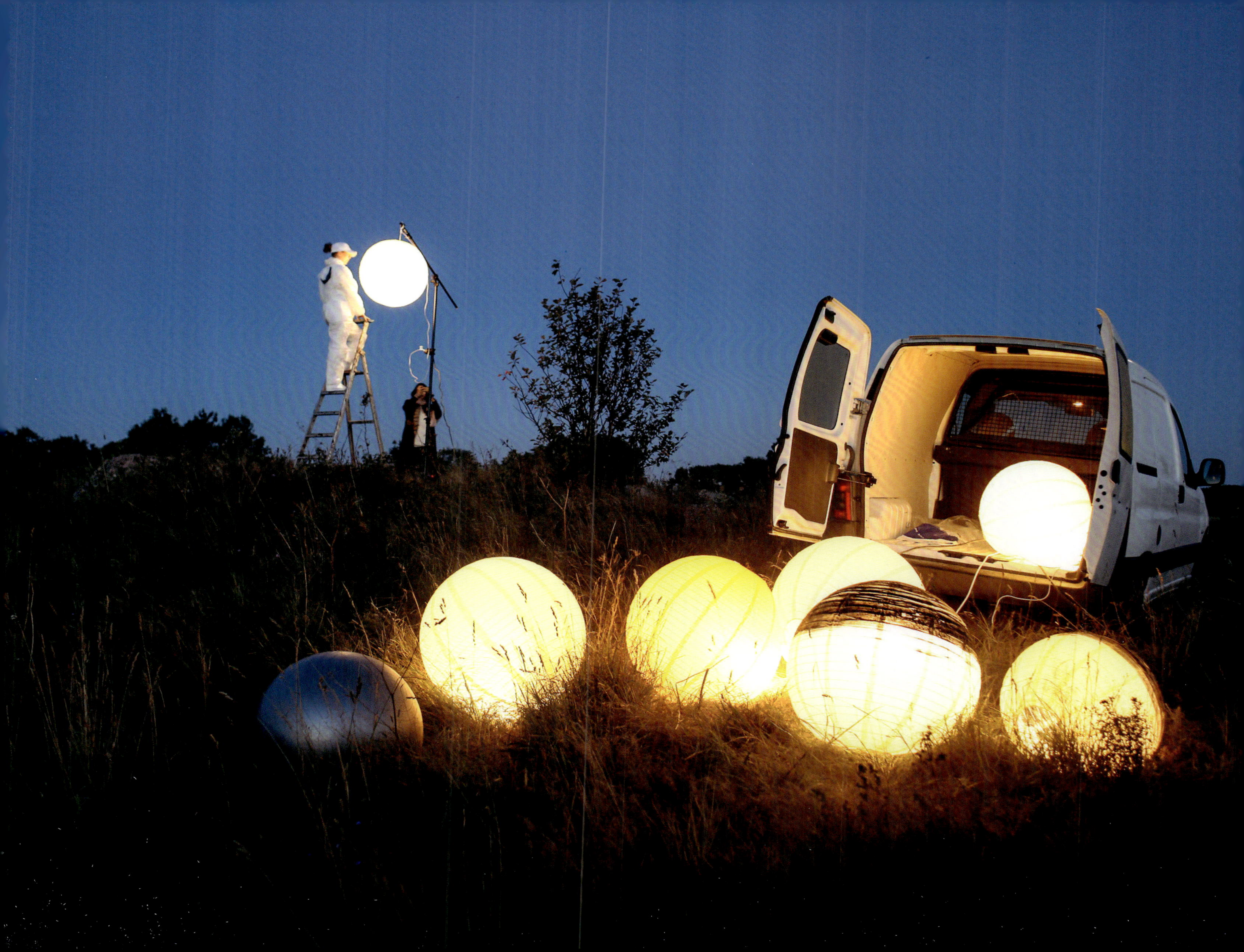

The concept for "Impact" emerged from the ideas that a calm lake resembles a mirror, and that nature is fragile. I wanted to create an image where a person – whether consciously or unconsciously – has ploughed their way through a lake, causing it to shatter like a mirror: a reflection on the fragility of nature and our lack of care for it. I wanted to capture the exact moment where the person realises what has happened.

I held on to this idea for a long time, until one day I saw an ad placed by a gym that was relocating and wanted to get rid of a bunch of large mirrors. I went there, bought four mirrors and took them to a glazier who cut them up according to my sketches. Then I took the mirror pieces along with a model and a canoe out to a quarry and photographed everything.

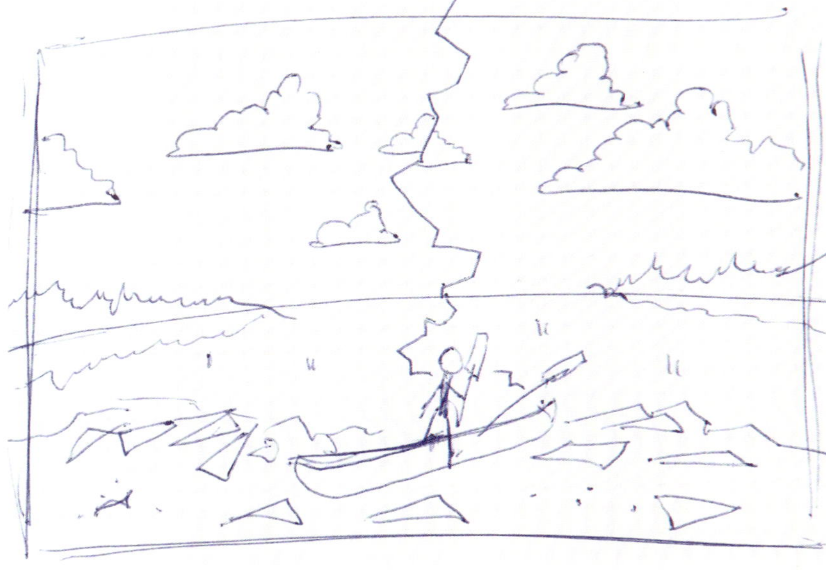

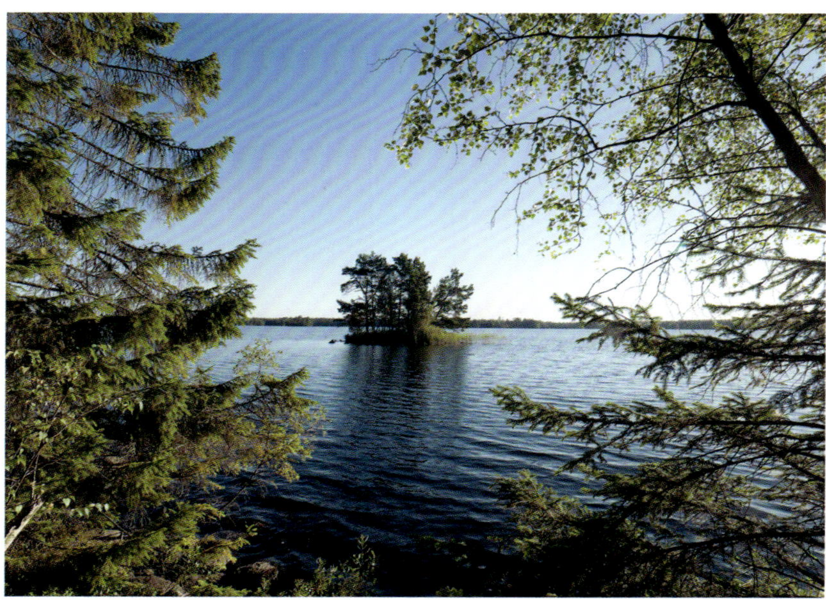

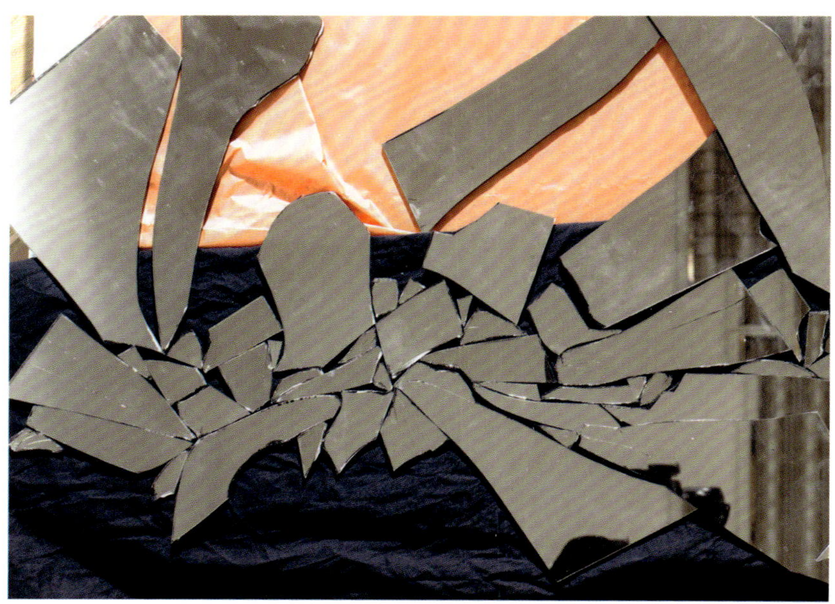

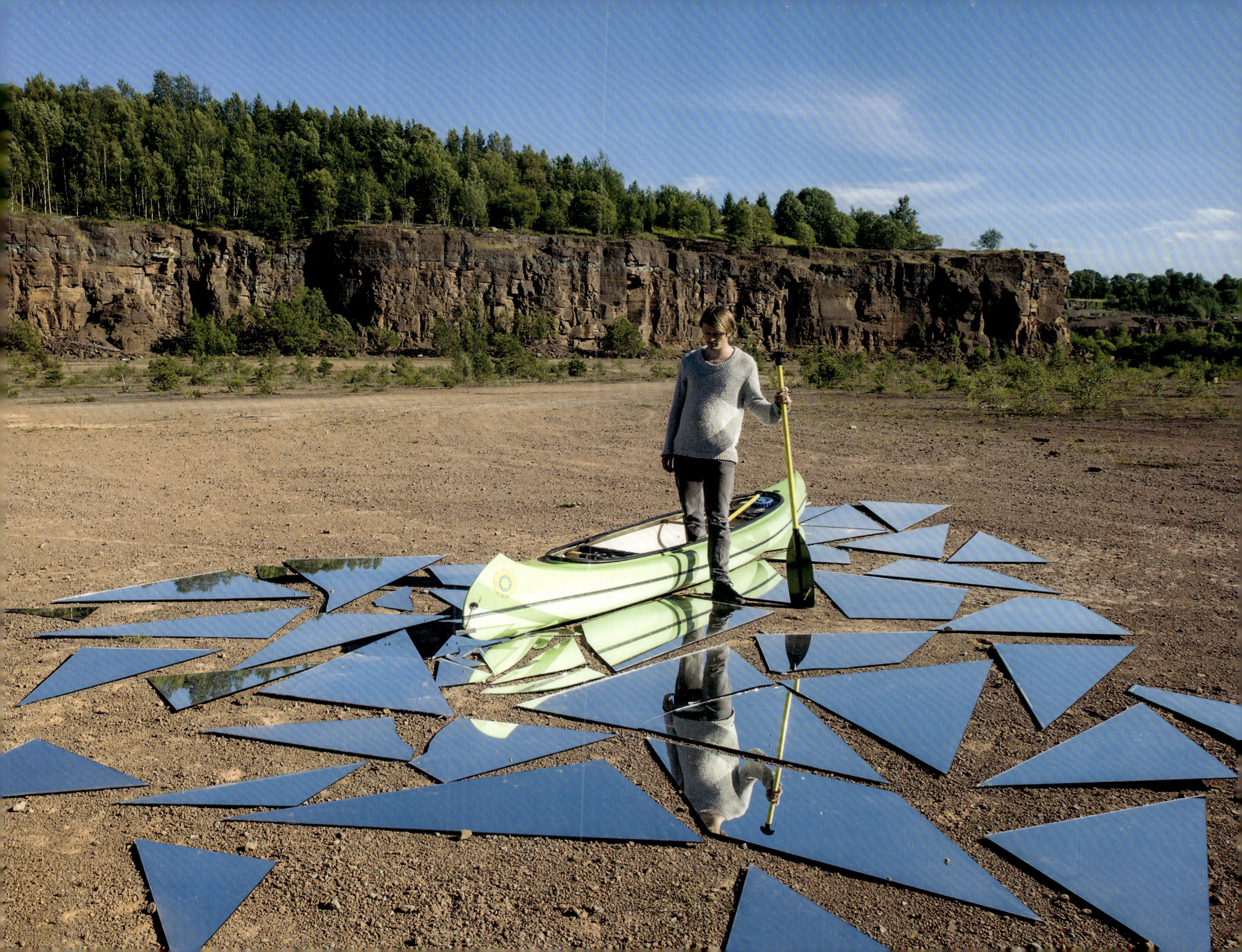

This image isn't necessarily about escaping from the office, more about being brave enough to step out of our familiar, safe surroundings into the unknown.

It has a symmetrical composition, with the corner of the office dividing the space in two. The left side symbolises the familiar and known, while the right side represents the unknown. The model is facing a choice between two ways out: the door to the left and the window to the right. He is already positioned somewhat to the right, as if he has already decided it's time to let go of his taped-together paper plane.

To create the dull office setting, I bought a piece of carpet and a used desk. I went to a film studio and rented an old computer and some other office equipment. Then I constructed a 2-metre-long paper plane out of heavy cardstock, which I then covered in old failed exam papers from my university years.

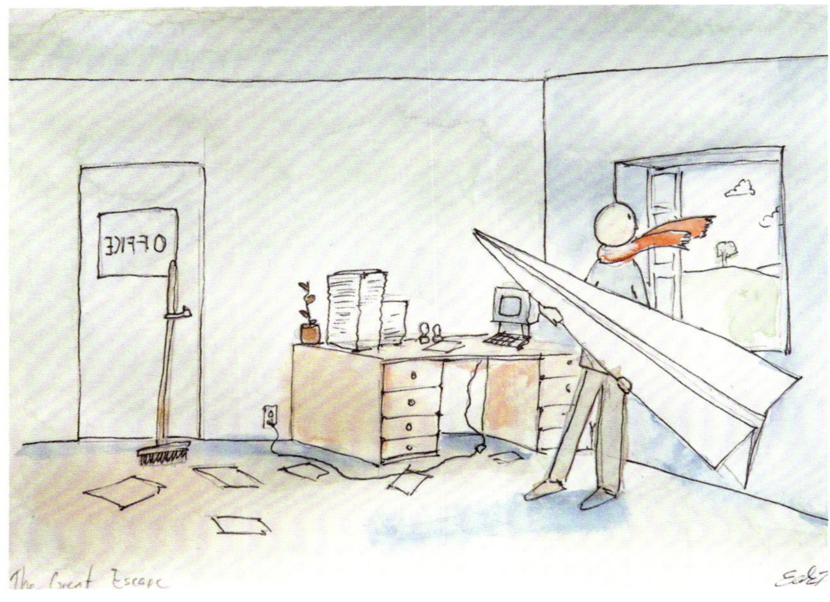

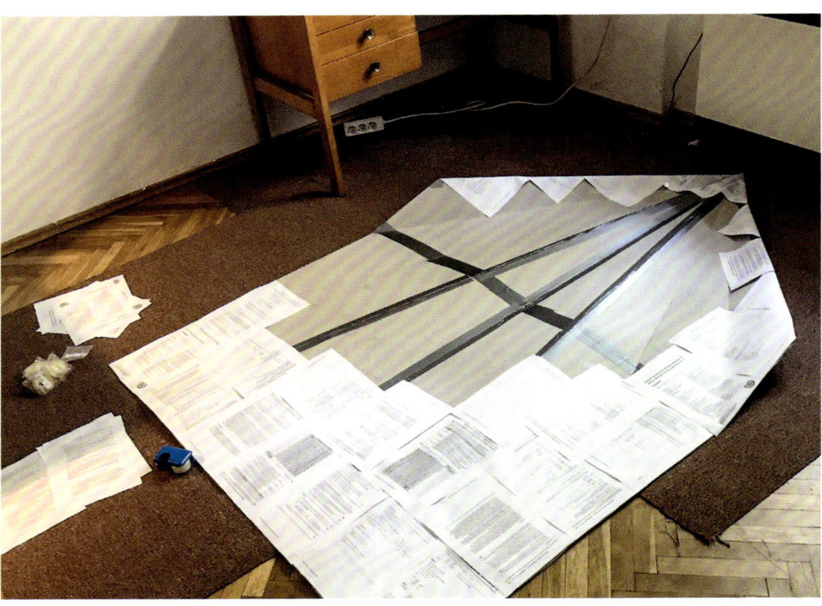

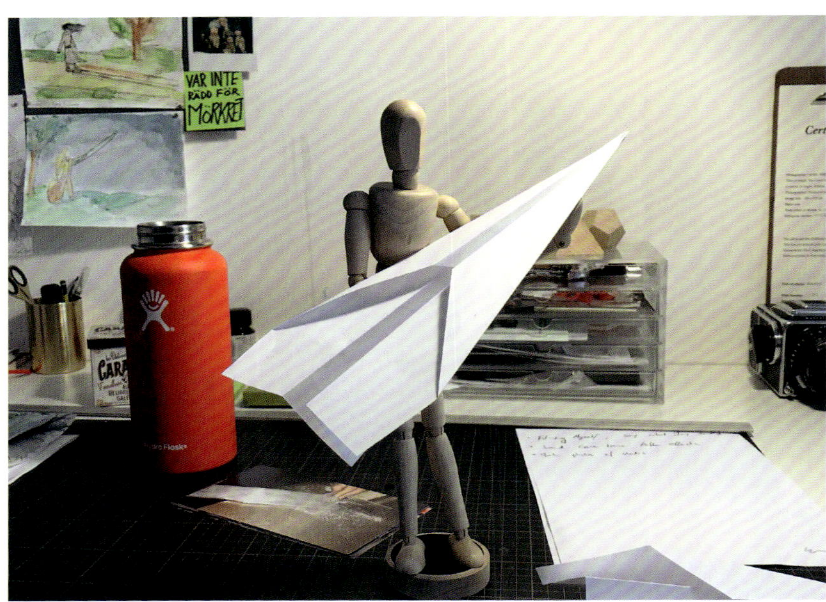

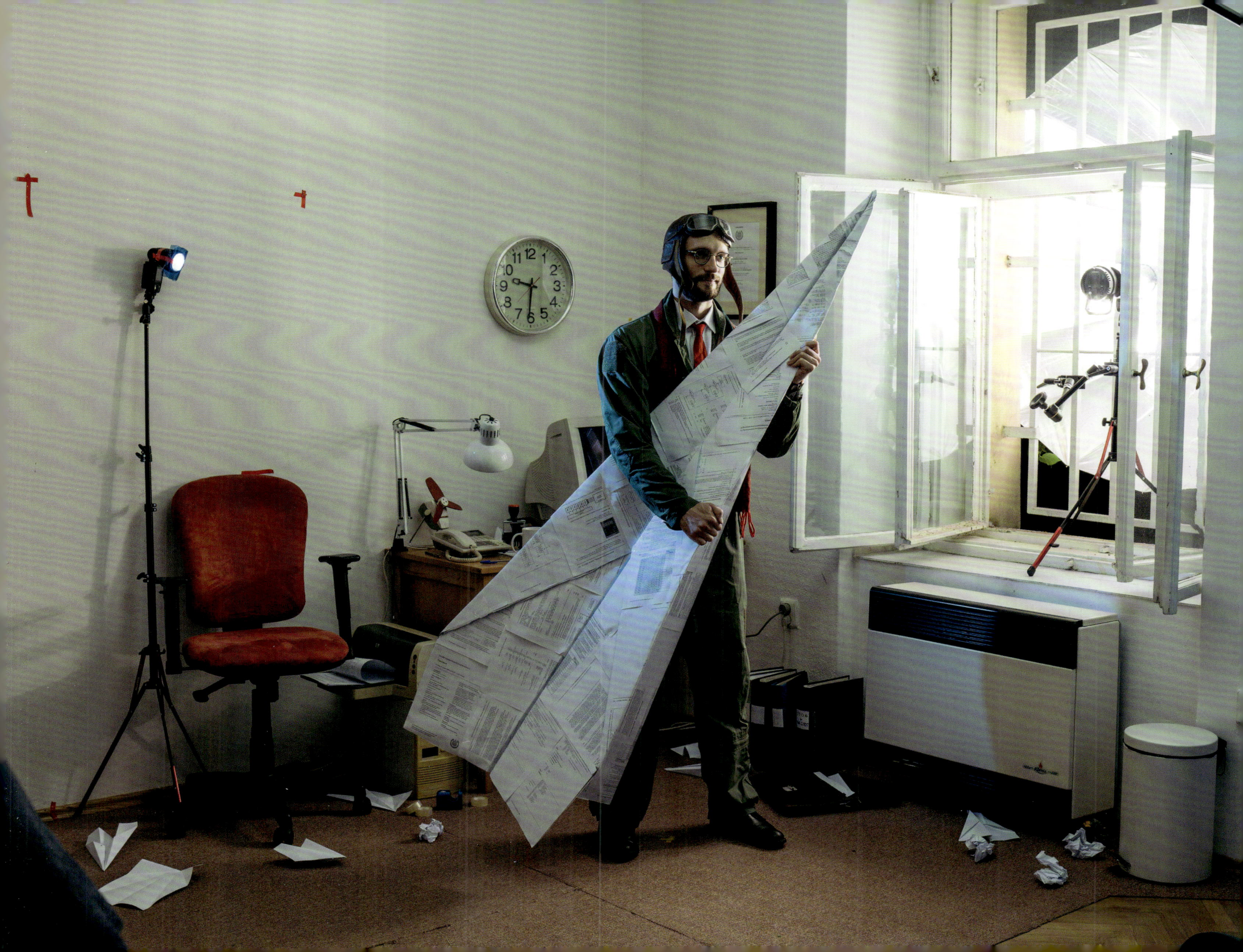

I've been fascinated by arches ever since a friend who was studying architecture told me about their properties. An arch is an amazing arrangement in which every stone provides support for the adjacent ones, thereby creating a stable curved structure. But if you just remove one stone, the whole thing collapses. I started thinking about a society structured along the same lines: about how we are not that strong individually, but together we can create something stable.

I photographed the background in the northern Czech region called "Bohemian Switzerland" one day in late October right after a rain shower. Then I sketched out the positions of the houses in the structure and realised their shapes would need to be modified somewhat so they would fit together perfectly. The perspective of the image meant I had to photograph some of the buildings from a higher vantage point and others from below. In the end, I used a combination of buildings from Prague and Stockholm.

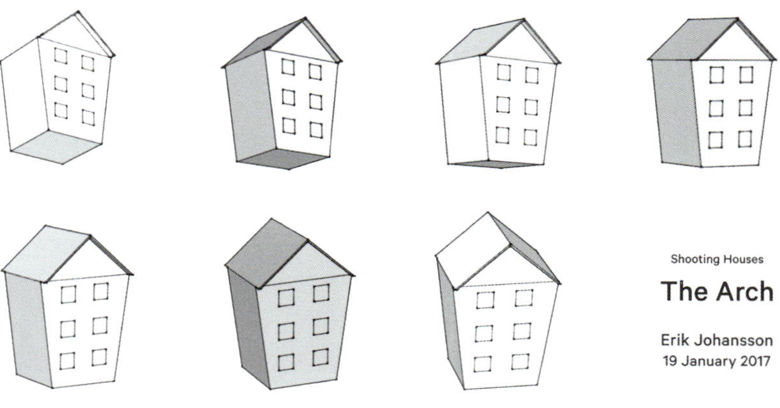

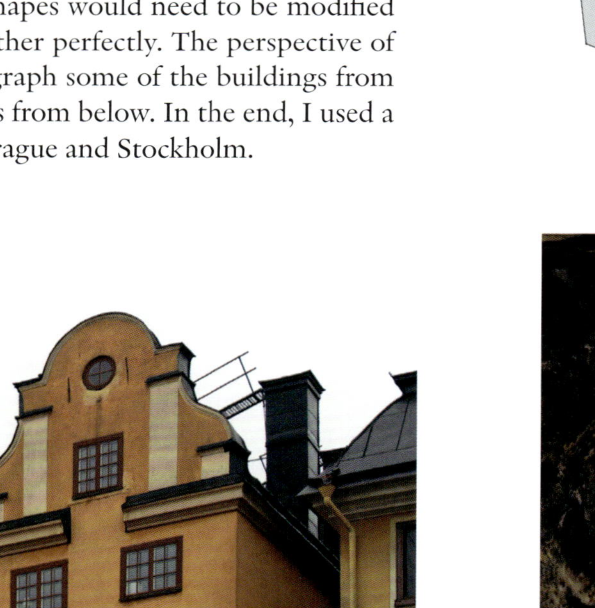

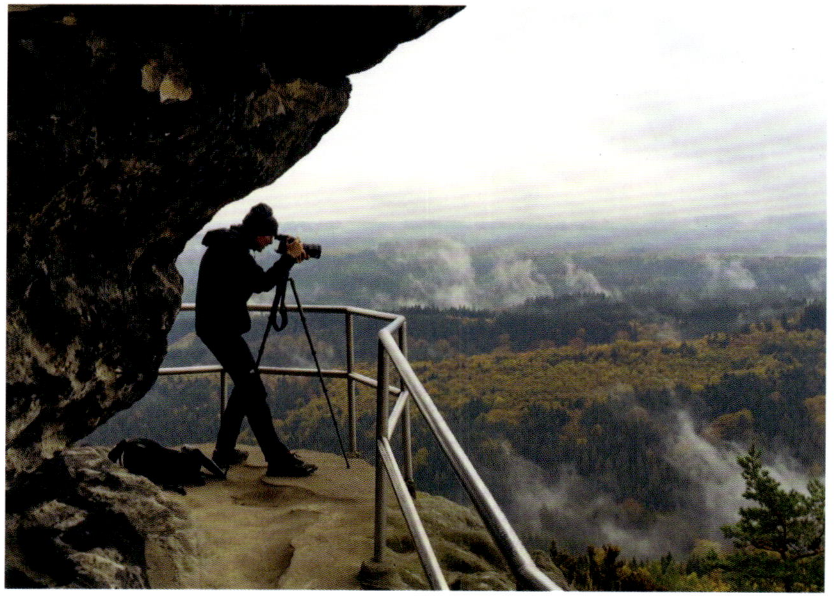

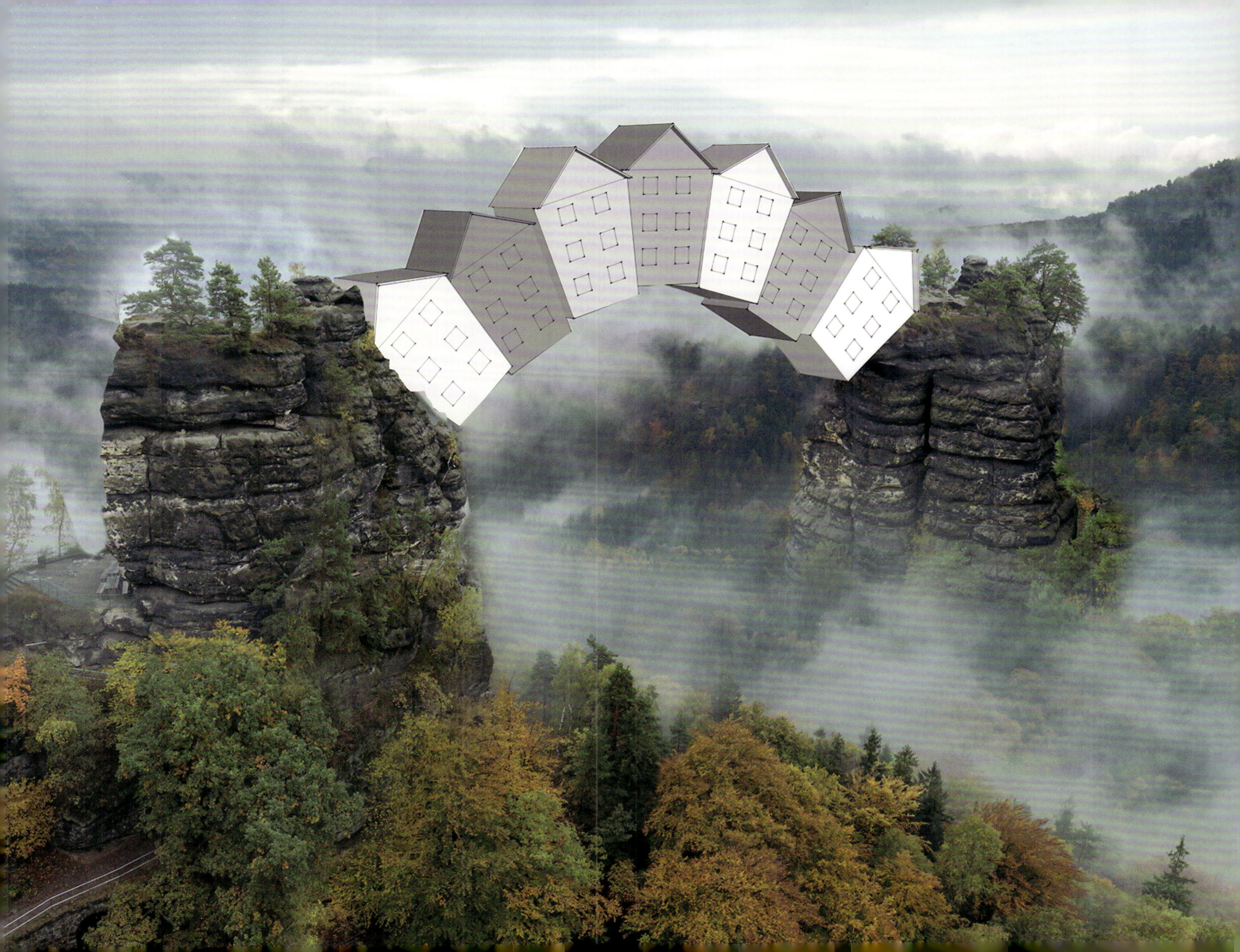

For a long time I had been thinking about a person who plucks stars out of the sky or places them up there. The sky is vast, so presumably they'd need some kind of tool to reach the very highest stars. Right away I thought it might be a sort of tongs or tweezers – something relatable. I couldn't find any giant tweezers, so I decided to get in touch with a blacksmith, who helped me construct some tweezers a metre and a half long in solid aluminium. It cost extra to get the ridged texture put on them, but I wanted them to be perfect, fully functional tweezers – just larger than usual.

Appropriately enough, the name of the model in this image is Stella (Latin for "star"). She works on films as a production designer, so she also helped with the design of the tweezers. We shot the image one evening in late summer on a rocky hilltop. A small flash was taped on the tip of the tweezers to cast starlight on the model and over her surroundings.

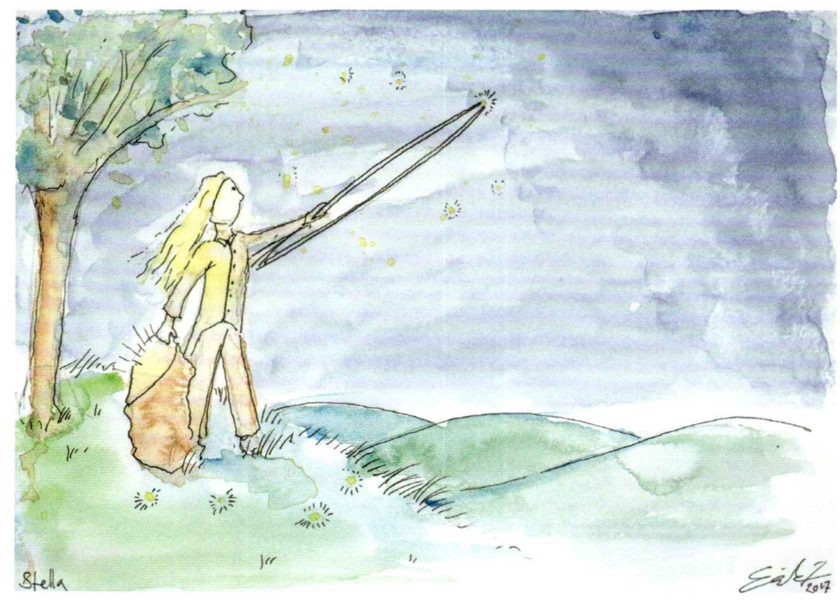

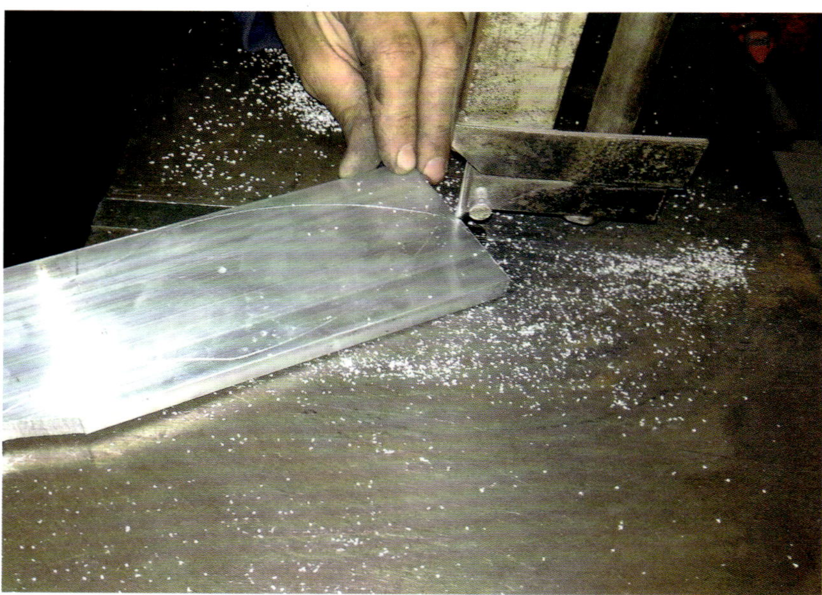

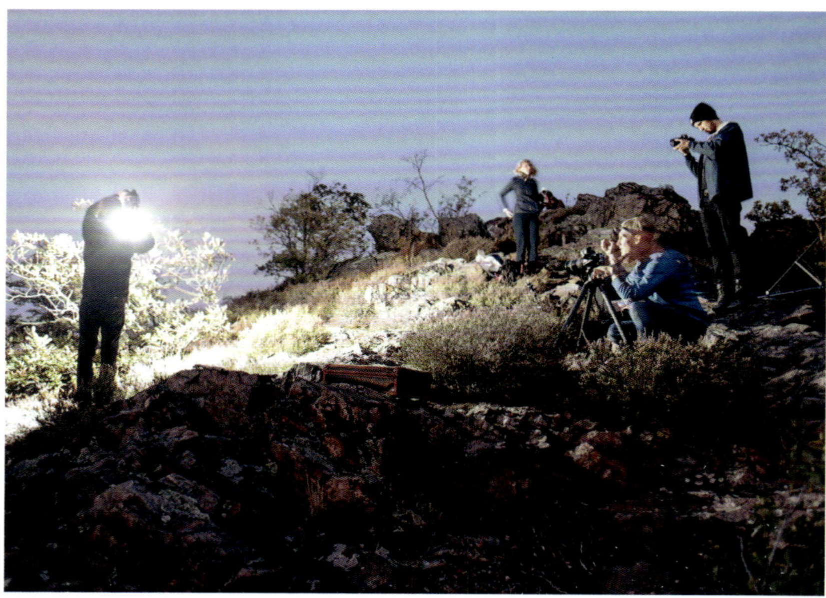

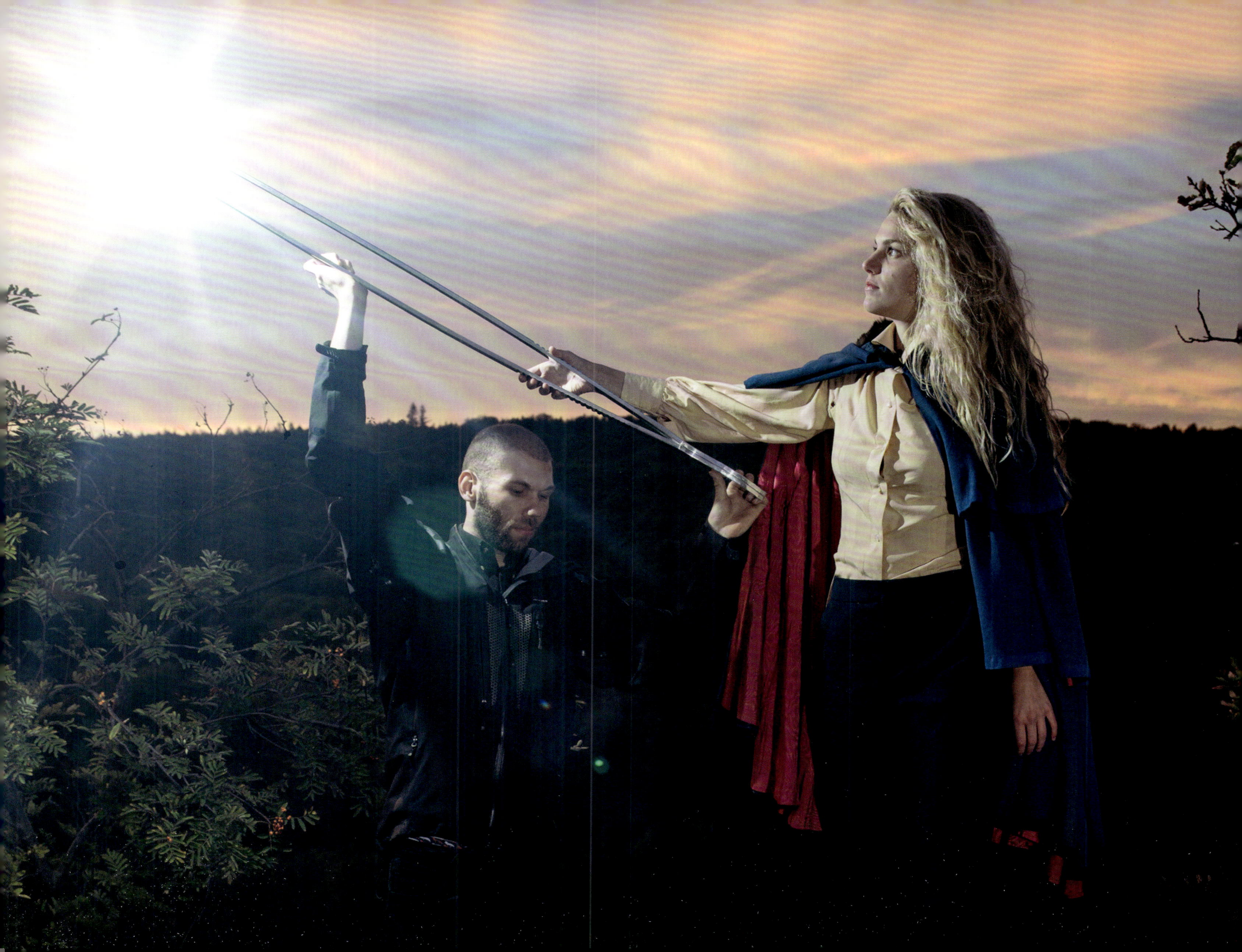

© Bokförlaget Max Ström, 2019
© Erik Johansson
www.erikjo.com
Translation from Swedish Ruth Urbom
Design Patric Leo
Repro Italgraf Media
Printed by Graphicom, Italy, 2022
Fifth printing
ISBN 978-91-7126-491-6
www.maxstrom.se